Buying, Selling and Moving House: The Complete Planner

Buying, Selling and Moving House: The Complete Planner

Kate Robertson
and
Gail Lawther

COLLINS

The Diagram Group

Editor	Denis Kennedy
Indexer	David Harding
Designer	Richard Czapnik
Design Staff	Joe Bonello, Brian Hewson, Carey Hunt, Philip Patenall

Consultants
Financial: Peter Robinson-Somerset & Co.
Legal: Peter Wells-Wells & Co.

First published 1987 by
William Collins Sons & Co. Ltd

Typesetting by Bournetype, Bournemouth

Printed and bound in Great Britain
by Billing and Sons Limited, Worcester

British Library Cataloguing in Publication Data

Robertson, Kate
Buying, selling and moving house: the complete planner.
1. House buying – England 2. House selling – England
I. Title II. Lawther, Gail
333.33′8′0942 HD1379

ISBN 0-00-410442-0

Foreword

So – you've decided to move house. Maybe you've moved before, and are only too well aware of the things that can go wrong, the possible hold-ups, the complex arrangements that have to be made. Even if this is your first move, you'll soon be regaled with tales of woe from relations, acquaintances and so-called friends who have been through the process themselves. Whatever your position is, *Buying, Selling and Moving House: The Complete Planner* is just the book you've been looking for.

Moving house is a serious business; enormous amounts of money are involved, and many careful plans need to be made. This book will take you through the process step by step, showing you just how to go about each stage, what the different options are, and how to make the right decisions that will most benefit you and your household. Money matters and the legal transactions and liabilities involved are clearly set out, and the numerous practical arrangements necessary are detailed with many helpful checklists and plans-of-action.

So often when you're moving one incident can mar the whole experience – a distressed and frightened child or pet, a removal van that fails to materialise, or a new property with no key available. If you work your way through *Buying, Selling and Moving House: The Complete Planner* you should be able to ensure that the hold-ups are kept to a minimum, and that moving is a pleasant, enriching experience rather than a nightmare one!

One important point worth considering before you start reading the text in detail is that the law relating to buying and selling property in Scotland is quite different from that which prevails elsewhere in the UK. If you are interested in property in Scotland, it is therefore advisable to consult **SECTION FIVE: THE LEGAL SIDE** initially, which will provide an indication of the main differences in procedure you are likely to encounter.

Contents

SECTION FIVE: THE LEGAL SIDE

SECTION SIX: PREPARING TO MOVE

SECTION SEVEN: THE DAY OF THE MOVE

SECTION ONE
WHY MOVE?

So – you are thinking of moving? And obviously thinking quite seriously if you have bought a book all about the process! If you're about to take your first step into property ownership it's good to realise that before reaching the satisfying position of settling down to your first cup of tea in your own living room there are all sorts of complicated decisions to make and procedures to get through. For those of you who are already owners but are now on the move again, you know only too well the potential difficulties involved. In both instances you can save yourselves a great deal of time and possible heartache by working your way through the varied advice on the following pages. There will be a lot of questions to consider and things to sort out, in particular your own priorities for your move, its timing, and the type of property you will be buying. All these things will need to be matched with your finances, the legal procedures involved, and the help of various experts such as estate agents, solicitors, surveyors, building societies, banks and removers.

Before you get caught up in the excitement of planning where you will go, how many bedrooms you want, and perusing dozens of local papers and DIY interior decorating books, ask yourself seriously – why do you want to move? You're about to embark on a major financial undertaking, not to mention possible frustrations over disappointing surveys, delays with long chains of buyers and sellers, rejected offers, and extensive sorting, packing and unpacking. You shouldn't move purely on whim or because you have had a slight tiff with your parents, (former!) friends, or landlady. You should have sound reasons for moving that will make you certain, through all the problems of the months to come, that it's all going to be worth it in the end. You may need to move nearer work, or require more space for a growing family or an elderly relative; you may be recently retired or disabled and need a smaller, easy-to-manage property. You may want to escape troublesome neighbours, in-laws, city smog, train noise, etc. To move just because all your contemporaries have a place of their own and you don't want to be left out is not a terribly good reason for taking on the burdens of home ownership.

House-hunting (and flat-hunting) takes time and energy, and some financial outlay even before you actually buy a property, when you think of fares, petrol, time off work, and surveyor's fees, not to mention maps, local papers, postage and so on. Sometimes house-hunters will find a house on the first day of looking, but more often it will take weeks or months; if you are particularly unlucky you may still be looking after a year or two if chains of buyers and sellers build up and then collapse. A mixture of determination and good fortune are required to keep you going when things get tough. And yet, when everything has finally fallen into place, when the removal men have left and you have unloaded the final box, you can then experience the excitement of a great achievement. And if it's your first house there is a wonderful sense of independence as you experience the freedom to choose what colours to paint walls, what and when to cook, how often to have a bath, and the heady sensation of using your own front door key to come home at whatever time you like!. And, whether it is your first or your fifth move, there is the chance of meeting new neighbours, establishing a new routine, finding new routes to work and exploring new shops and local facilities. Perhaps this is daunting to some people, but others thrive on the idea.

For some people a move is essential, indeed forced; perhaps job relocation requires it, or the unexpected arrival of triplets when you were planning on a single child changes your plans. For other people retirement could bring a wish to settle in a warmer, prettier part of the country, or deciding to work from home could require space for an office or workroom. In all these cases you will want to use the most effective method of choosing what you want, finding it, financing your purchase, seeing it through legally, and finally arranging and completing the move itself. All of these aspects of home buying are dealt with in this book, and there are all kinds of hints, checklists and diagrams to help make the whole process easier. Buying a house is a complicated process, but by working your way through the various stages step by step the whole business can be made less traumatic. Happy house hunting!

Buying versus renting

You may want to move and have very valid reasons for doing so. But do you have to *buy* a property: what about simply renting a house or flat? Thousands of people are quite happy to pay a council or a landlord a sum each week or month for anything from a bedsitter to a large house. On the Continent renting is usually the norm, with many people never really considering buying their own place; both cost and convenience mean that they are happy having other people looking after repairs, decoration, maintenance, etc. So what *are* the advantages and disadvantages of owning your own place?

Two factors seem to sum up the attraction of buying: independence and investment. As regards independence, there is no doubt far more freedom in having your own house than in living in one owned by someone else. You can choose what to do with the property in the way of decoration, upkeep, facilities, furnishings, when to carry out repairs, etc., and whether to extend or alter the house. You can keep pets, build cupboards, put in nails to hang pictures, repaint, and generally make your own decisions. Furthermore you don't have to pay out rent week in week out with little say over what the money is spent on. You don't have to share a bathroom or toilet with someone you hardly know, or return by a certain time each night.

Conversely, if you aren't inclined towards DIY or don't notice decor particularly, or if you work long hours and eat out so that you're hardly ever at home, then there seems little point in buying just for the sake of independence. If you see your home as a place purely to sleep and for cooking the odd meal in then renting has some attractions. You have few if any unexpected bills and so household budgeting is straightforward, and you have no responsibility to arrange repair work. As rented accommodation is usually furnished, you don't need to pay out for fittings and furniture. You will have periodic contact with the landlord over the odd problem – for example, a rent query, leaking tap or faulty electrics – but by and large if you pay the rent promptly and stick to the rules you will be left fairly well to your own devices.

Yet, many people will tell you that if you can afford to buy you should buy. And, certainly, there are advantages in home ownership. Most of all property ownership is a relatively safe form of investment. In general, over the last decade house prices have kept well up with, and sometimes outstripped, inflation. In areas of increasing population and high demand for property, especially in the South-east of England, prices have soared ridiculously. There is no fixed guarantee that prices will keep on rising, but what better options are there for investment? Cash devalues, stocks and shares may rise but can plummet, investment accounts can be profitable but you pay tax on the profits. Once you buy your own property you have a good capital investment and even if the selling market does sink, or reach a level plateau, you at least have a place to live in. You can stay put for as long as you like, unlike in rented accommodation where you might be asked to leave after a particular period or if the landlord decides he would like to live in the property himself.

People often comment that with renting you pay out for years but at the end have nothing to show for it. Why not pay a building society instead of a landlord, and in 25 years' time have your own place? This is a reasonable point, but remember that there is no disgrace in renting; it can be a serious option to consider. Renting can also be a short-term option to help you to save up money for a deposit on your own house; in this way you may be able to save on your eventual mortgage in the long term. Also, if you're newly married or just making your way in your chosen career, renting can free you from the worries of house decoration and maintenance when you'd rather spend your time on something else. However, an increasing majority of people in this country are attracted to the idea of home ownership, and this is what this book will be dealing with.

One final thought, though. Before you decide definitely on purchase, remember that it is not all simplicity and light. Buying is a complicated business, and added to this is the problem of the capital outlay at the start long before you are likely to see any return on your investment. You will be committing yourself to a set minimum outlay every month. Subject to fluctuations in the interest rate, for the next 20 or 30 years, and you are taking on the risks of theft, damage, repair bills, etc, which will now be carried by you rather than a landlord. So, you might decide to buy, but how much can you really afford at this stage? We'll be looking at costs and financial options later in this section.

Timing and possible delays

One of the most frustrating things about the whole moving process can be the timing. Friends will alternately bore you and horrify you with stories of how they bought and moved in within a few weeks, or how they had five house deals fall through at the last possible moment! Others will tell you that they looked for three years before they found a suitable property... It's impossible to give an exact time-scale for your personal schedule, from the day you decide to move to the day you actually manage it, as there are so many variables and so many different people involved.

The first variable is property availability. If you are looking in a crowded popular town or city any accommodation coming onto the market can be snapped up almost before the particulars are issued. Alternatively, in depressed areas many people could be selling up to go elsewhere, and so you might be able to pick and choose. Sometimes, often for no apparent good reason, certain areas become *the* place to live in a town; prices soar, and you can't get a look in unless you're prepared to pay well over the odds.

The next variable is the 'house chain' – the sequence of buyers and sellers with which you are involved. Here first-time buyers, and buyers of new homes or new conversions, are at a distinct advantage. The house chain builds up when each person who is moving into a new property is dependent on the present owner's move, who in turn is waiting for the owner of his intended property to move, who in turn... and so it goes on. First-time buyers are popular because they rarely hold a purchase up, as they have nowhere to sell. They either stop paying rent or move from living with their parents, and can generally adapt to sudden changes in procedure quite satisfactorily. If you're buying a new home from a builder your main delay could be that the building firm was too optimistic with a completion date – you may find that the roof still isn't on when you want to move in. In cases where you have to sell in order to be free to move – even when that is the limit of the 'chain' – you could take only days or many months to find your buyer, depending on the state of the market, the desirability of your property, the number of other similar properties available, whether your asking price is realistic, and so on.

The present social climate brings in yet another possible delaying factor. Divorce is becoming increasingly common, and house sales often follow as a result of a marital split. Procedures can then be held up as financial settlements between the partners can be subject to lengthy debate. It's worth checking, tactfully, why the house is on the market; checking through your solicitor may be most effective, as he or she will have access to the seller's solicitor. Illness, redundancy and bereavement are also unforeseen factors which can alter your original plans for buying and selling.

The other key variables are all to do with the professional help you will be enlisting and the legal, financial and surveying procedures. By and large there are general guidelines proposed by solicitors, building societies or banks and surveyors regarding the length of time they expect their part of the process to take, these are laid out diagrammatically on the next two pages. However, as people (and other unpredictable factors!) are involved, don't expect everything automatically to flow smoothly. You yourself will be involved in arranging meetings, being available to talk with people or view houses at particular times, forwarding documents and keeping the pressure on if things aren't happening. Your solicitor may be in a busy period with other things happening: there might be legal complications over the property you are going to buy; a legal search might reveal that the house is under a compulsory purchase order; your survey might reveal that it requires major work, or is subsiding; the mortgage firm might have numerous applications to consider, or be in a lean time for lending money and granting mortgages ... and so on.

You might have found all these rather negative emphases alarming or depressing. To an extent we have deliberately stressed the things that can go wrong, simply because it's best at this stage to be aware that problems can and do occur at different times and places in a complex process. The prime variables are the time taken to sell your own property and the time taken to have an offer accepted on a property which suits you and is a good buy. Obviously if it's important to you to move by a particular date, for instance if you are starting a new job or the school year is beginning, the pressure can be great as you try to ensure everything is done within the necessary period of time; occasionally, unfortunately, things don't fall into place and other plans have to be made. However, assuming that all goes reasonably smoothly, the flowchart overleaf shows the average time taken by the various stages in buying a house.

The standard time-scale

This flowchart will give you an approximate time-scale for completing a standard house purchase and assumes that you are only buying, not buying and selling, property. This time-scale is the minimum that can be realistically expected; most sales take longer, and some may stretch into months (or even, if you are spectacularly unfortunate, years). Even if the sale goes through with no major hitches, there may still be niggling little problems such as delays with the searches, hold-ups from the seller's solicitor in replying to enquiries from your solicitor, delays from the building society or bank in making the money available, etc. There is generally a gap of about four weeks between exchanging

Week 1

- Put in an offer on property
- Offer is accepted by seller
- Inform seller's estate agent
- Inform your solicitor of the intended purchase
- Apply for a mortgage to building society or bank
- Organise a building society or bank valuation for the new property
- Your solicitor asks for a draft contract from the seller's solicitor
- Your solicitor sends searches and other enquiries to local council, etc.

Week 2

- Your solicitor receives draft contract from seller's solicitor
- Your solicitor sends a list of enquiries on the details of the contract to the seller's solicitor
- Your building society or bank inspects the property

Weeks 3-4

- Your building society or bank agrees the mortgage you require
- Search enquiries are answered satisfactorily
- Seller's solicitor and your solicitor agree terms of contract
- Satisfactory survey confirmed on the new property
- You sign the contract, and make out a cheque for the deposit

contracts and completion, so by the time you exchange contracts you should be able to fix a moving date that suits all parties.

Remember that as well as the procedures shown here you also need to fit in your own planning – for instance, clearing out your attic and shed, doing any work that needs to be done on your present house, sorting out new schools for the children and informing the authorities, notifying the gas, electricity and telephone people of your requirements, choosing and booking a removal firm or self-hire van, sorting out someone to look after children and pets, etc. Work your own schedule out to coincide with the legal schedule as far as you practically can.

Weeks 5-6

- Your solicitor is instructed by building society or bank, and prepares conveyance
- Your solicitor sends draft conveyance to you
- Your solicitor requests cheque from building society or bank by a certain date
- Your solicitor and the seller's solicitor exchange contracts (probably by post)
- Your solicitor calculates stamp duty, fees, etc, and gives you notice of how much money will be needed to complete the sale
- You sign conveyance and mortgage agreement

Weeks 7-8

- You or the bank/building society, send the cheque for required amount to your solicitor ready for completion
- Your solicitor receives the cheque and has it cleared in the usual way
- Your solicitor receives a clear search certificate
- Your solicitor orders a bankers' draft or prepares a telegraphic transfer ready for completion

Weeks 9-10

- Completion; your solicitor stamps the conveyance and mortgage, sends the deeds to the building society or bank, and you take possession of your new property.

Mortgages: general considerations

Even though you want to move, and maybe a change in location is necessary for work or family reasons, there is one big question to answer before you ring up the estate agents. Can you actually afford to buy a property? This isn't a question to brush off lightly. The reality today is that an ever-increasing number of houses are being forfeited as mortgage repayments fall behind. This is not only because of unemployment or a drop in income; often people have been caught up in borrowing money for things to fill the house on extended credit without thinking through the consequences. Some people fail to understand that if they can't afford something now they are unlikely to be able to afford to pay out over forthcoming months at often crippling rates of interest.

So, do be warned. As you read the advice on gauging what you *can* afford, bear in mind other expenditure and what your standard of living costs are now. Think carefully of what your standard of living is likely to be in the future (for instance, are you expecting a baby, or a pay rise, or are you just about to buy a car?), and also decide what standard of living you are prepared to tolerate (are you prepared to give up foreign holidays, or eating out?). Be realistic as you assess your income, prospects and lifestyle, and you should be able to find a property that you are financially as well as physically secure in.

Most people have to borrow money to buy a property. Only a few people have saved, or inherited, enough money to buy outright, and even if they have they may choose not to pay the full sum immediately; the government gives some support to borrowers for property-buying in the form of tax relief. Sources of borrowed money, and more of the intricacies of borrowing, are written about in more detail in **SECTION FOUR: FINANCING YOUR PURCHASE** but at this stage we'll assume that you are hoping to borrow from one of the main building societies or a bank. By the end of this section you should have a fair assessment of what price property you can look for, linked with a general assessment of your income and outgoings (ie, discovering what money you will have left over to pay a mortgage). In effect you will be answering many of the questions that a building society manager will ask you when you apply for a loan. He or she will be very keen to ensure that you are realistic in your assessment, because of course the building society stands to lose money if you get into financial difficulties. Be honest as you answer the questions, as you will only be cheating yourself if you don't. It's tempting to claim a higher income than you actually have so that you can get a higher mortgage and buy a more expensive

property, but remember that the reason for linking the mortgage available to your income is so that you can have a rough-and-ready guide as to whether you can afford the payments. If you make false claims, it is extremely likely that you *won't* be able to afford the regular payments. The amount a society is prepared to lend you is based broadly on your income and your financial commitments. The society expects you to repay each month for a period of years (determined between you, but it could be as short as 5 or 10 years or as long as 25) a proportion of the sum borrowed and part of the interest on the loan. Exactly what you pay off will depend on exactly what kind of mortgage you take out.

Neither of you can determine what disasters might overtake you in the years during which you are paying off your mortgage. Risk of death needs to be covered by an insurance policy, while long-term illness, disability, accidents or unemployment are less easy to allow for. These are all parts of the risk of taking on a mortgage, unless you are prepared to pay for extra insurance policies to cover such eventualities. By and large, though, you will expect your income to rise slowly; if you can afford a certain level now, the future should be assured (barring the events mentioned above) provided that your other expenditures don't go out of control.

One point is very important to couples, and deserves careful consideration before you decide how much you can afford. For couples buying together, if both partners are working building societies can allow a percentage of the second wage-earner's salary to be taken into account when the mortgage is assessed. But if you plan to have children, remember that you will lose one wage during the time that one of you stays at home to look after the children. Even if that partner then returns to work, there will still be large extra bills to pay for childminding, and extra food, clothes and equipment for the children. Take these factors into account if you are moving into a bigger house so that there will be room for children; the last thing you want to do, with the increasing responsibilities of a larger family, is to find that you have over-reached yourself financially.

How much can I afford to repay?

The sum you are trying to arrive at is the amount that you can set aside each month, out of your income, to pay off a mortgage. First of all, you need to start with your basic income (or incomes, if there are two or more wage-earners in the household). At this stage you can get a rough estimate of the amount you may be allowed to borrow by multiplying the higher of the two salaries by $2\frac{1}{2}$ and adding $\frac{1}{2}$ of the lower one; this is only a rough and ready guide, as different societies and banks have different policies, and there are also other factors to be taken into account, but it will give you a starting point.

You might also have other sources of income as well as your basic wage. Do you regularly earn more with overtime, or regular bonuses, or private work, or commission? What about government-paid allowances such as pensions, disability allowance, attendance allowance, etc? Some of these are tax free, but their status can change with successive governments, so assess whichever ones are considered taxable income. It's worth noting that the building society or bank will generally want a written confirmation of your salary from your employers, especially if you are applying for a first-time mortgage. This is standard procedure, so don't take offence that the society or bank wants to check. On the 'negative' side are outgoings, both regular and occasional. Do you have any regular HP payments to make – on a car, TV, video, washing machine, etc? Do you have any dependants or maintenance payments: Self employment can be a problem if you are just starting off working for yourself; your income is less likely to be regular, and can make assessing your incomings and outgoings rather more difficult. Building societies and banks like ideally (some insist) to see the most recent 2 or 3 years of accounts to make sure that you are a reasonable risk for a loan.

These points cover most of the things that a building society or bank will want to know; for your own personal assessment of your financial commitments, you will want to be a little more detailed. You don't need to become obsessive about every little penny, but jot down roughly how much per month you spend on food and drink, clothing, household expenses, travel (including car maintenance and petrol, insurance, etc), insurance policies and pension schemes, medical and dental fees, leisure, hobbies and entertainment (including TV licence and club memberships), gifts to church or charity. Also check with a home-owning friend the rough amounts you'll be likely to spend on fuel and telephone bills (this sounds tedious, but it's worth knowing the worst at this stage!). These sums added together give your expected monthly expenditure. Now divide your income by twelve, and subtract maintenance and HP payments and your monthly expenditure. What remains is a rough estimate of the amount of money you will have free for a mortgage and for one-off expenses such as holidays, and items for the house such as a new set of curtains or a dining table.

If things look bad from this rough calculation, then you may need to reassess your living style for the first years you pay a mortgage. Do you cut out cigarettes or have fewer trips to the cinema, or will you have cheaper holidays until you have a pay rise? Could you get by with a bicycle or public transport for a while, rather than paying out on a car straight away? Only you can make the choice of how to adjust your standard of living; in many instances buying a home calls for a few sacrifices at first. In order to assess your outgoings, work out each figure per month (or assess for the year and divide by 12).

Outgoings	
HP payments	
Entertainment	
Food and drink	
Clothing	
Household expenses	
Dental fees	
Travel	
Car expenses	
Insurance and pension schemes	
Leisure and hobbies	
Any other outgoings	
Total Outgoings	

Income	
Basic salary after tax	
Any other salaries coming to the household	
Bonuses, overtime, commission	
Allowances (eg child benefit, attendance allowance)	
Any other income	
Total Income	

Total Income	
Total Outgoings	
Amount left for mortgage and one-off items:	

Initial costs

By this stage you will have a good idea of what sort of accommodation you can afford, and a rough idea of the price range you can afford, related to your regular income. However, the actual process of buying, moving and setting up home requires a fair-sized capital outlay even before you begin paying off your mortgage. Though on paper you might be just able to afford a small property at £25,000, you need to pay a number of fees for services, and spend out money to make the place as habitable as you want it to be from the start. It's dangerous to stretch your finances to the limit right at the onset in case unforeseen circumstances arise or you have to sell your present property for well under your asking price.

Deposit

You will almost certainly be thinking of financing your purchase, partly if not wholly, through a mortgage. Only occasionally is it possible to obtain a mortgage which covers 100% of the purchase price, and this is usually only available for first-time buyers of new properties; more often the rule is that you will need to put down a 5% or 10% deposit, and this will be one of your biggest initial expenditures. Obviously, the higher the price of the property, the more readily-available funds you need to have. (This is looked at in more detail in **SECTION FIVE: THE LEGAL SIDE.**)

Decoration and furnishings

The next potentially large outlay is harder to assess, as it will depend on the condition of the property that you end up buying and also the speed at which you wish to carry out alterations, decor changes, etc. You may buy a property with the intention of adding on a granny flat before moving in fully; obviously this will add to the cost considerably. You may be buying a property with carpets and curtains included in the price, but you might still wish to provide your own; you may also want to paint or paper over the previous owner's choice of wallpaper or emulsion colour. It's rare for successive owners to have exactly the same taste, but remember that cosmetic work of this kind doesn't have to be done straight away; you can make do for quite a while and just tackle one room at a time, as long as the place is habitable. Things such as poor plumbing, rewiring, re-roofing, etc, are obviously more important and more urgent. Furnishing can be an enormous outlay, but once again don't get ensnared in the trap that you must have everything straight away, brand new. A cooker, bed, fridge, and a simple table and chairs, are virtually the only real essentials for civilised living in a new property; things like a washing machine, freezer, new 3 piece suite, stereo, microwave, matching crockery, sideboard and built-in wardrobes are all things that can wait until you can fully afford them.

There can be no simple guideline to the amount you will need to set aside for improving your new property; it will depend on what resources you have available, what furnishings, etc, you already own, and the state of the property you are buying. Assess the first two factors as closely as you can before you begin property-hunting, and then bear the third in mind as you look at different properties for sale.

Legal fees

Generally, people hire a solicitor to see them through the relatively complex legal requirements involved in property purchase. There are no set fees for this work, but usually relate to the house price, and are usually between ½ and 1% of the purchase price. There are extras as well: stamp duty is paid to the Inland Revenue on a property whose value exceeds a certain price (£30,000 at start of 1987); the exact price at which stamp duty becomes payable varies with different government directives. A land registry fee is also payable and a search fee. All of these are covered in more detail in **SECTION FIVE: THE LEGAL SIDE.**

Surveyor's fees

You will always have to pay for a simple valuation of your new property carried out on behalf of the organisation supplying the mortgage; this is not an extensive check, and the fee is not large (around £50 for a £30,000 property), but is necessary to reassure them that they are not paying out on a bad investment. You may also wish to pay for a private, more thorough, survey. Remember that if you come close to buying several properties without managing to complete a sale, you will have to pay out for several surveys.

Removal fees

Whichever way you choose to move, either by hiring a van and moving yourself or by paying a specialist firm, there will be some costs involved. These will vary of course, depending on how much you have to move and how far you are going; if you are moving a family's goods and furniture any distance you will need to think in terms of at least £200.

SECTION TWO

DECIDING WHAT YOU WANT

What part of the country will you move to? This is one of the main questions to answer. Perhaps you are moving because of work? Your firm or office could have relocated, maybe in one of the new towns where councils encourage development at cheap rates, and you have to move or else change jobs. Or perhaps you have just landed a good job too far away from your present home to commute. Maybe you have recently got married and now the two of you are trying to decide where to set up your first home. Or maybe you've retired, and are looking for a home in a pleasant environment, with no particular ties to work or area. You could consider somewhere very local, close to family and friends, for a first home or a retirement house, or you may be adventurous and want a fresh start in new surroundings. You may need, for financial reasons, to move to an area where property prices are cheaper.

Whatever your reasons for moving, and no matter how near or far from your present area you end up, some of the principles remain the same. Before you go out hunting it's good to establish in your own mind what your ideal property is likely to be, and then what facilities you would like to have nearby. From there you can adapt this 'perfect' picture to list essentials relevant to your household (such as 'three or more bedrooms', or 'large garden'), and non-essentials (for instance 'near a cinema' or 'facing east/west rather than north/south'). You need to be realistic; it's unlikely that you will find a property that corresponds with your dream in every particular – if you do, you will be unlikely to be able to afford it! – but it is helpful to narrow down in your mind what you are looking for in general. Couple this picture with what you can afford and you should be able to approach an estate agent with clear guidelines, and save yourself a lot of time by not having to wade through piles of particulars on totally unsuitable properties.

In your thinking, do allow room for forward planning; ie, not only what would be nice for the immediate future, but also whether the move is going to be short-term or long-term. Are there any foreseeable changes in circumstances that need to be taken into account in your choice? For example, are you planning to have children? If so, how many? (Remember in this that things don't always go according to plan; you may end up with significantly fewer or significantly more children than you planned!) Will any job promotion require more entertaining in later years? Will any relatives be coming to live with you, or staying for long periods? If you buy a large property or garden that requires a lot of maintenance, will you still have enough free time or energy to do the work required in a few years' time? Although a property on three different levels may seem quaint now, will you feel the same if your arthritis gets worse? A property by the sea may give you beautiful views, but will you be able to take an influx of tourists year after year? What do you intend doing in five or ten years' time? If it's significantly different from what you are doing now, for instance a total change in career direction, will the same property still be suitable? If you have several teenage children living at home, how much longer will they be there? Maybe you could let out rooms to students when your own children have left home, or have the house divided into flats and sell one off. Think these things through; many people spend only a few years in a property before feeling they need to move because of changed circumstances, but some of these moves could be avoided with a little forward planning.

The rest of this section details the vast range of options available to you when you are buying a property. Many of them you might not have thought of, or might not have considered as relevant to you; take a good look at all the options, as there might be factors you haven't taken into account in your first thoughts on the kind of home you would like. There are numerous checklists to help you sort through and assess your priorities and choices. If you are choosing where to move as a couple, it's a good idea to photocopy some of the lists and complete them independently first of all; then get together, compare notes, and work out areas of compromise! And if you have children in your household, do let them give some input into your decisions. Make sure that they feel fully involved in this major decision, as in many ways the move will affect them most. It's probably better to get them used to, and excited about, the idea of moving early on, rather than springing a sudden change on them at a later stage. Moving can be a chance for all the family to feel that they will gain something; abstract ideas such as 'we'll have a nicer house', or 'we'll be closer to the station' don't hold much sway with children. Changes that relate to their world will mean much more to them: 'we'll be nearer to grandma and grandpa', 'you'll be able to have a playroom', 'we'll have a bigger garden, so you could keep rabbits/birds/a dog or have your own bit of garden to grow whatever you want'. If they can see reasons such as these for moving, they'll be much more likely to anticipate the change with pleasure rather than dread.

Which area?

Once you have settled on the general part of the country you're moving to, you need to decide next which particular area of it will be best for you. If you are able to buy a property outright, for instance if you have been left a lot of money or if you are buying a small property to retire to, then you may be able to choose a property in any reasonable part of your chosen location. Most people, however, will be bound very much by work considerations.

You need, of course, to have a regular source of income to pay the mortgage on your new home, so unless you want to spend considerable time (and money) commuting, you will want to live as close as possible to your place of work. If you are self-employed or can work from home then your options are probably wider, but you still may need to be near a station or within easy reach of the town centre. If all your work is at home, then your priorities will be more for space for a study, studio, workroom, etc.

Assuming, though, that you travel to work each day, your first choice of area will be related to easy access to your workplace. Unfortunately the choice is not always straightforward, especially if you live in the South-east of England. In recent years a great disparity in price has arisen for similar properties in different parts of the country. For the price of a four-bedroomed house in parts of Wales or the North-east of England, you could scarcely buy a one-bedroomed flat in London; the same amount would provide only the deposit for a house of the same size in the fashionable environs of London. In these circumstances you have a difficult balance to sort out. The further from your place of work you go, the greater the cost of commuting. However, the cost of living very close by could be prohibitive because of the property prices. You therefore have to find the optimum distance from your workplace where property prices are relatively low and the cost of commuting, in time and money, is not too prohibitive.

One factor that can work in your favour when you're working towards this kind of balance is that in many larger towns and cities property prices vary somewhat from area to area and even from street to street, depending on whether the particular area is currently fashionable. Look out, therefore, for pockets of cheaper property within the same region. Do check, though, just why certain areas are particularly cheap; there may be some rather unpleasant reason, for instance, because it's the red light district, or because there is a high incidence of violent crime.

Having narrowed down the general area, move on to the other considerations concerning your way of life and the specific

amenities you require – or would like ideally. Once again, these will, of course, vary with your particular household and lifestyle. If you have children you will want schools within easy reach; if you are very athletic you will want a sports centre or facilities nearby; if you are musical or keen on the arts you will want to be near a theatre or concert hall. If you work from home but use the post a lot, you might need to be near a main post office; if you require lots of deliveries of raw materials, you will need a property that is easy to find and not too far off the main thoroughfares.

You'll also need to think of shopping facilities. Small local stores are very handy, but are generally expensive. If you're not near the centre of a town, maybe there's a superstore in the locality that you could load up with once a month, and just use the local stores for small items. Do you need to be near a doctor, dentist, dispensing chemist, osteopath, etc? What about religious beliefs; is a good local church important to you?

Only you can decide exactly what amenities you require and how near-by or far away they can be. Only you, too, can decide what is essential and what is just desirable. There will inevitably be a measure of compromise as, of course, you are very unlikely to have everything you could possibly want on your doorstep. Even if things aren't close at hand, good public services can make them readily accessible; are there good bus routes nearby? If there are, and if there are also good quick roads into your nearest town or shopping centre, it won't matter so much if you have to travel a little to reach some of the facilities. Be realistic; having a property in the country with a 'local shop' mentioned on the estate agent's particulars is fine if the shop is good, the road to it is well maintained, and the distance is only a few hundred yards. On the other hand, if the shop is simply an overpriced sweetshop, a mile away down unmade, unlit roads, this will be a very different proposition.

On the next two pages are checklists for you to fill in to help you work out what your own priorities are for your new property, and also to use as master lists when you are looking round possible properties.

Area checklists

How far do you want to travel?
Study the table below and tick the distance you would ideally wish to travel from your dream home to the corresponding

My dream home	**0–½** mile away	**½–1** mile away	**1–2** miles away	**2–3** miles away	**4+** miles away
bus stop					
train station					
postbox					
post office					
bank					
library					
shop					
shopping centre					
good supermarket					
playgroup					
infant school					
junior school					
middle school					
sixth form college					
good church					
park					
playground					
cinema					
theatre					
concert hall					
sports hall					
pub					
restaurant					
hospital					
doctor					
dentist					
health clinic					
....					
....					

facilities. Then take photocopies of the table below, fill one in for each new property you view, and then make a comparison with your dream home.

Property

....

0–½ mile away	½–1 mile away	1–2 miles away	2–3 miles away	4+ miles away	
					bus stop
					train station
					postbox
					post office
					bank
					library
					shop
					shopping centre
					good supermarket
					playgroup
					infant school
					junior school
					middle school
					sixth form college
					good church
					park
					playground
					cinema
					theatre
					concert hall
					sports hall
					pub
					restaurant
					hospital
					doctor
					dentist
					health clinic
					....
					....

What kind of accommodation?

Once you've decided on an area to move to, you need to narrow down just what kind of property you're looking for. Remember that lots of people do end up buying property that doesn't correspond very closely to their original idea, and are very happy in it, but it will make your life (and the estate agent's) a lot easier if you have some basic ideas when you begin looking. The major requirements are those that are least likely to change – for instance whether you want a bungalow, or whether you want a garden; some of the lesser details are just to give you guidelines to think along. Many of these can be altered by you once you are in the property in any case; for instance if you want a property with central heating you can always buy one without and install it; if you want a utility room you may be able to build one on to the property. Of course, though, it's always satisfying when the property you buy corresponds quite closely to your original ideal.

Type of property

You will need to decide whether you are looking for a flat or maisonette (which you will probably have to buy leasehold) or whether you definitely want a house – ie, a property with no-one above or below you. If you want a house, do you specifically require a bungalow, or do you want to be on two or more levels – or don't you mind either way? Houses can be terraced (attached to other houses on each side), semi-detached (attached on one side only) or fully detached – although, especially on modern housing estates, you might find that 'detached' actually means 'a hand's width away from your nearest neighbour'! If you or your family will be producing a lot of noise, for instance if you play musical instruments, or run a noisy playgroup or club from your home, it might save problems in the long run if you buy a detached house, or a semi-detached one where the main rooms are farthest away from your neighbours. If you are very adventurous you may even be thinking of building your own home, either as part of a housing association or to your own plans. If you are elderly and finding your present accommodation too much to handle, you may be considering moving into sheltered accommodation, where there is always a warden on call to help in difficulties.

Age

Are you hoping to move into a new house or an older one? Both have their pros and cons, of course. Newer houses are more regular in shape and size than very old ones, and so easier when it comes to things such as replacing windows or fitting curtain rails. They are also less likely – though not, of course, totally exempt – to develop problems such as damp, woodworm, rot, and so on, during the time you are in the house. Brand new houses should also be covered by building certificates, which will give you some protection should any of these problems occur. Older houses, on the other hand, tend to have more character, both in the house and in the garden. Maintenance may well be more expensive, though; older houses were not built to the same stringent regulations that are currently in force in this country, and so may tend to be prone to problems from the minor to the major.

Size

Estate agents usually use the number of bedrooms you require as a rough and ready guide to the kind of property you are looking for, so work this out, taking into account whether you want a permanent guest room, intend to take in lodgers, or will need an extra room upstairs for a playroom, workroom or study. Then decide how many bathrooms you will need, and how many toilets. If you have small children or elderly relatives, it might be important to have a toilet downstairs. If there is only one toilet in the property , it's best to have it separate from the bathroom so that people can occupy the bathroom without needing to worry about anyone wanting to use the toilet. Next work out whether you need any extra space for things such as a utility room, a space-consuming hobby or collection, a music room or studio, a study or sewing room or workroom, etc.

Outside

As well as deciding what you want inside the property, you need to decide a few details about the outside. Do you want a garden – and if so, what size can you cope with. If you're interested in gardening you may want a sizable garden with lots of different features; if you're not, or don't have time, you will want one that requires as little maintenance as possible. What will you need in the way of garages, outbuildings, sheds, and so on? Think now, too, of whether you'll be looking for a property with room to extend in later years; if so, you might want a big garden so that you can spare some of it for building work. If you have small children, check the safety level of the garden; can they easily escape onto a busy road? Is there a pond they could fall into: Might stray cats and dogs come in easily and worry them?

Accommodation checklist

Your basic requirements
Use the questions on this list to work out the kind of property you would ideally like to move to. Don't stick too rigidly to every detail – get a general picture, then adapt as necessary if you see a property that you like and that seems basically suitable.

		What would you like?	How many toilets?	How many bathrooms?	How many bedrooms?
Flat/maisonette					
House:	Detached				
	Semi-detached				
	Terraced				
Bungalow:	Detached				
	Semi-detached				
	Terraced				

Do you want sheltered accommodation?		Yes	No
Which area?	Rural	Yes	No
	Urban	Yes	No
	Residential	Yes	No
	Shopping	Yes	No
Does it matter if the house is on or near a main road or railway?		Yes	No
Would you like to buy a brand new or modern house? If not, what kind of period would you prefer? (eg, Georgian, pre-war, Victorian, etc).		Yes	No
Do you need a garage? If so, what size?		Yes	No

If you have children, what features are needed for them? (eg, playroom, reasonable garden, no open-plan stairs, not too many different levels, etc).

....

....

If you are elderly, or will have elderly relatives living with you or visiting frequently, what features are required? (eg, bungalow, no parquet floors, draught-proof windows and doors, etc).

....

....

Do you need a downstairs toilet?	**Yes**	**No**
Any other special rooms needed – eg, study, utility room ?	**Yes**	**No**
Anything you need extra space for? (eg, collections, a large freezer, washing machine and tumble dryer).	**Yes**	**No**

What size garden would you like?

....

What kind of garden would suit you best? (eg, mainly lawn, orchard, shrubs, vegetables).

....

What outbuildings would you like? (eg, shed, greenhouse, stables, etc).

....

What other features would you like ideally? (eg, central heating, gas cooker, immersion heater, double glazing, plumbing for a washing machine, a patio for barbecues, a balcony, etc).

....

....

Seeing possibilities

Before you limit yourself to only one type of property, based on your immediate short-term needs, it's worth thinking ahead a little. Moving is a complicated and often trying business. Many people move again and again as their personal circumstances change, and each move brings its own stresses, yet many of these changes in lifestyle are predictable in advance. A frequent reason for moving is because people find that they haven't enough space for a growing family, an elderly relative living in with them, or workspace for someone who has decided to become self-employed. Some people find that as their work responsibilities increase they need more space for working at home, or for entertaining. These demands might mean that you require one or more of the following: another bedroom, a study, a workroom, another (or larger) reception room, an extended kitchen, a self-contained flat within or attached to the house, a downstairs toilet or even bathroom.

However, moving to another property is not the only option open to you. More and more people are choosing instead to extend or alter their present property – or to move once to a property with possibilities for extension or alteration. So it's a good idea at this stage to think about how you expect your life to go in the next five or ten years. Possibly you could choose a property with potential for you to build on to at a later stage – both when it becomes necessary and when funds are available. In this way you could save much of the hassle of moving – and swap it instead for the different problems of having builders in the property! The advantages, though, are obvious; children wouldn't need to be uprooted from school, you can still be in the neighbourhood you enjoy, and you won't have wasted any money or effort you've spent on the property up to that stage. Rather than having to look all at once for a very large property that encompasses all the space you might potentially need, you can adapt bit by bit as the finances become available. Basic structural work can be done first, and decoration and equipping later.

You do need planning permission for most extensions. If they alter the outside look of the property you need council approval. Inside work needs to meet building regulation standards, which are generally related to safety. If you are inclined towards DIY work, you need to check that what you want to do is safe and up to standard. But what kind of property should you consider? Obviously if you know that you will want more space downstairs, for instance for an invalid relative who can't climb stairs, or for an enlarged reception room for entertaining; then you will need a garden or patio area to build on. Alternatively, you may find that you could convert a garage into a room – in this case you will need somewhere else to park the car, and also to keep all the odds and ends currently in the garage!

If you're looking for an extra bedroom, playroom, workroom or study, this can be upstairs or downstairs. One popular place to expand is the attic; you can have a loft converted in various different ways (once again a conversion will need to meet fairly stringent building regulations). If you have a garage built on to the side of the house, you may be able to have a room or two built over the top. If you are having an extra bedroom (or two) added, do remember that you may well need another bathroom as well. If you want a completely self-contained flat for a relative such as a parent, or maybe a newly-married son or daughter who can't yet afford to buy a property for themselves, you may find it preferable to have the flat detached from the main house. In this case you will need a large garden, or a property with a basic outhouse such as a double garage or workroom, which can be converted into a flat.

Not all extension work needs to be a major building undertaking. If you simply want a space that is private, for instance for a workroom, music studio, art studio or study, you may find that one of the ready-made sheds or conservatories serves the purpose. For instance if you were setting up your own business painting watercolours, a ready-made conservatory added on to the back or the side of your house would provide weatherproof space and light for a fraction of the cost of building an extra room.

Have a long, hard think about the space you might require in the next 5 or 10 years, and use the chart below to jot down possibilities for extending your present property or a not-so-large new one; list the particular features that would be required and consider also the space available (eg, large garden, sizable attic, room to build over the garage, etc).

Possibilities for extension

What kind of feature is required?	What space is available?

Buying your own council house

If you are currently a tenant of a council house or a related housing association house, and have been a council tenant for a total of two years or more (not necessarily consecutive years), you are entitled to buy your council house. Your local council offices will have the full details in their literature, but these are the rough guidelines.

If you have been a tenant for two years, you are entitled to a discount of 32% on the market price of your house; if you have been a tenant for 30 years or more, you are entitled to a discount of 60%. These discounts mean that the rent you have paid while a tenant will, in effect, be considered as making the first payments towards buying your house. The types of housing that will be taken into consideration towards your discount entitlement are not limited only to straight council housing; they include years spent living in armed forces married quarters, and time spent in a variety of other tied housing; full details are listed in the councils' literature. If you are living in a flat or maisonette, you can buy a long lease instead of buying the freehold of the house.

Of course, once you buy your house you are committing yourself to becoming fully responsible for rates, water rates, house insurance, and repair and maintenance, as well as for your mortgage repayments. There will also be several one-off fees just as there will be if you are buying a private house – land registry fees, valuation and surveying charges, solicitor's fees, etc. If you meet the requirements for being entitled to buy your house, the relevant council or housing association is obliged to give you a mortgage, even up to 100% in most cases, if you wish. However, you may well find that if you can get a mortgage from a building society this will work out cheaper, so explore all the possibilities. Some building societies will give 100% mortgages for buying council properties, but others prefer you to put down a deposit yourself. If you can't afford to begin paying a mortgage straight away, you have the right to delay your purchase for two years from the date of your application to buy. If you do this, the price and the terms will remain the same as at your date of application.

It is also possible for you to buy the house in conjunction with any other joint tenant in the house – for instance if you have been sharing your council house with your spouse, or with a grown-up son or daughter. Any number of joint tenants can take part in the purchase if they want to. If they don't want to, they will be required to sign a form saying so; they will then lose their tenancy rights in the house when the sale takes place. If you can't afford the total sum for your house, you can opt for the Shared

Ownership scheme, in which you will become part-owner of the house and the rest will be considered as rented.

Exceptions

Generally speaking any council or housing association tenant that meets the residential requirements is entitled to buy. There are, however, a few exceptions.

- If your housing association was funded by public subscription, you may not have the right to buy; the same is true if you live in almshouses. You must rent your home from one of the landlords known as the 'Right to Buy Landlords'; these are listed in the relevant literature.
- If you are living in housing specially set aside for the mentally ill or the mentally handicapped, or sheltered housing intended for handicapped or eldery people, you may not buy. Also, the property must be a self-contained unit, so, for instance, if you have a room in a council hostel this will not qualify you to buy no matter how long you have been there.
- If you have a house that has been specially adapted to suit you as a handicapped or elderly person, at the time of writing you do not have the right to buy, but much debate is currently raging over this exclusion.
- If you are living in housing which is temporarily occupied pending redevelopment by the landlord, this will not qualify.
- If you have been squatting in a council property, but have since been given official licence to occupy the property, this will not qualify.
- If your property is within the boundaries of a school, cemetery, social services home, etc, this will not qualify.

There are some other fine points relating to certain conditions in which the right to buy does not operate; these are detailed in the leaflet *Your Right to Buy Your Home*, available from council offices.

Selling

Generally, once you have bought your council house you will have the right to sell it to anyone you choose, at any time. However, if you sell within five years of buying, you might have to repay some of the discount you were entitled to at the time of purchase. If you have bought a property on a national park or other area of particular beauty, you may find that you can only sell to a buyer approved by the council – which will generally mean anyone other than a property developer!

Buying a new property

One option worth considering in your search for a suitable home is that of a brand new house or purpose-built flat. We have all driven past the new housing estates with their 'Show house open for viewing' signs, while all around workmen are trying to complete the rest of the houses. There is no doubt that in the early stages the appearance of such a housing plot can look bleak and rather characterless, but the show house will usually be furnished to present the chosen style of house to the best possible advantage. More and more people are finding the purchase of a brand new house perfectly satisfactory.

For a start, you have the opportunity to stamp your own personality on the decor without having to cover over the previous owner's migraine-inducing wallpaper of violent puce paint! As you are the first owner the house should be in pristine condition, both structurally and cosmetically; the place should be completely clean, and with nothing left hidden or forgotten in attics, sheds, under-stair cupboards, etc. There should be no stains from cigarette smoke on the ceilings, no grease marks in the kitchen, no childish graffiti in the bedrooms. But the most attractive thing of all is the reassurance of structural safety, shown by a National House Building Council certificate.

With older properties there is always a slight risk of structural fault not being spotted at sale, which then leaves you with no recourse to the previous owner to offset your heavy bills. Houses built by firms registered with the NHBC have to meet a stringent set of requirements in order to receive approval on design, correct choice of materials, and finally, actual craftsmanship in building work. All reputable builders are registered members, and any properties they build will be sold with a ten-year guarantee. For the first two years the builder is obliged to put right, at his expense, any faults arising from a failure to comply with the NHBC's building standards. You should make a list of any faults you notice as they occur and contact the builder to point them out. Small surface drying-out cracks in the plaster are not really the builder's responsibility – these are inevitable – but large settlement cracks are another matter! Should the builder go out of business during this period the Council itself should cover the costs. For the rest of the guarantee period the Council undertakes cover for major structural defects only up to a maximum of £100,000. This allows for problems such as subsidence, roof collapse, etc.

One interesting development during the last few years has been in the variety of options regarding facilities ready-supplied in the new house. These can start with a simple choice of colour of bathroom suite, walls and kitchen flooring, through to more elaborate choices of fully-fitted kitchens, fitted wardrobes, and carpets and curtains throughout. Indeed some firms now do special 'packages' for newly-wed or newly-retired couples. Here the builders not only provide the shell of the building, all the decoration and bathroom and kitchen equipment, but also all the furnishings and general fittings such as bookcases, shelving, dining table and chairs, beds, etc. You provide ornaments and luxuries – and yourselves! Naturally the prices of all these facilities are built in to the overall price of the property, but if you're not at all interested in fitting out your home, or don't have the time, they can prove a practical buy. Of course, you do run the risk of moving into a house or flat that is an exact counterpart of the ones next door, but as all these residents inevitably make their own marks on house and garden these similarities will become less obvious.

One person's joy could be another person's bugbear, and this may well be true of one aspect of your brand-new property: the garden. As the builders eventually move out, having completed not only your property but all the others and the connecting roads (and if you are one of the first to move in, be prepared for building work to go on around you for quite a while longer), you will notice the paucity of shrubs, trees and flowers. Some builders will plant trees, shrubs and even bulbs on common land, but most will leave the private gardens to the residents. Occasionally you will find a housing estate where the builders have established the houses and gardens around existing trees, but this makes building work less straightforward, and most builders prefer to start with completely bare land. So, the chances are that your garden will be totally devoid of plant life, apart perhaps from a lawn. For the keen gardener this is a lovely chance to establish from scratch the landscape of his or her choice, without having to dig out old plants and reorganise rockeries. For the unenthusiastic it can be a nightmare trying to establish lawns and flower-beds and perhaps get a little shade, or privacy. In either case, when you look at the price of the house remember to add on a realistic amount for putting in shrubs, trees, bulbs, etc, and possibly laying a lawn – and don't forget the amount of time it will take you, either. Also check, if you can, what the soil is like in the garden before you buy; if you are unlucky, you could find a sprinkling of soil over rubble and concrete.

Self build

In this modern era of self-help groups and workers' cooperatives, it should come as no great surprise that there is one further option in house buying: a number of people are involved in co-ownership associations and self-build societies. It is possible, of course, to have a home designed and built for you, or even to build part of it yourself, but in a group there are particular advantages.

A self-build housing association is a temporary grouping of people who aim to pool their different skills relevant to house-building and associated activities – for instance, plastering, carpentry, etc. Together they prepare plans for suitable accommodation and present them to a building society to borrow money for land, building equipment and materials. The members of the association then work together either full-time or part-time (as other demands on their time permit), and build the houses for each other. When all the work is completed each member applies for a mortgage on his or her individually-allocated property, putting the money into the common pool to pay off the initial debts of land and materials. When all the debts are paid off the association is wound up.

There are obvious advantages for a group over going it alone. First of all you are unlikely to have all the skills yourself to construct a property and see all the plans through the relevant channels, so you would need at various stages to pay for expert help. In a group you may find that you can summon between you all the necessary skills for basic house construction that you can then use cooperatively: plumbing, wiring, carpentry, bricklaying, concrete mixing, plastering, and general muscle power, not to mention the possibility of including architects, lawyers, town planners, etc. Furthermore, as a group you are often well equipped for raising finance and having the skills and the time available for negotiating for land.

The process

Naturally the procedure for building your own property will vary in many details from ordinary negotiations for purchasing and funding a property. The rough stages that will need to be worked through if you are thinking of going about providing a house for yourself in this way are the following:

- Think through carefully the skills that you and your household can offer, and make a realistic assessment of the amount of time you will be able to devote to a project such as this.
- Choose a group that combines a wide variety of skills and to

which, as far as you can tell, all the members are truly committed.
- Form a steering committee from among these members; the steering committee will do just that – steer the direction of the rest of the group.
- Agree on basic plans for what the group wants. Don't go into too much detail at this stage, for instance whether you are going to plant trees in the gardens; stick to issues such as what accommodation are we aiming for, and of what kind (eg, detached houses, a small terrace, a courtyard with housing round it and a communal garden, etc).
- Negotiate raising finance.
- Acquire a plot of land with planning permission, or negotiate the two simultaneously.
- Agree on, and submit, architect's plans.
- Acquire the necessary materials and equipment.
- Begin and complete construction.

It almost goes without saying that you do need to be fully committed to join a group of this kind. Complications of an horrendous nature could occur if people start pulling out, or quarrel, or become ill, part-way through. All these possibilities need to be covered in your basic agreement; no matter how amicable and committed you all seem at the beginning, it is possible for things to turn sour. You need a resilient nature; self-build opens up the possibility of far more delays, revised plans and schedules, unexpected events, etc, than ordinary property-buying. You are giving your time free, so all the members of the group will need to be seen to be pulling their weight. It's well worth finding and talking to others who have done this to discover realistically what strains and stresses may occur; they can also give practical advice on how to save on materials and architect's plans, basic house designs that can be purchased, etc.

An organisation worth contacting for further information is The Housing Corporation, details of which are given in **Useful addresses** (pp. 188–189).

The pitfalls of buying older property

Most people buy a property that isn't brand new; generally a house will have had one or two previous owners, if it isn't all that old, but sometimes it will be a much older property that may well have passed through dozens of owners. If you are buying a home that is anything more than about 20 years old there will be all sorts of problems to look out for.

Some older houses have always been looked after with great care, and you may find nothing worse than general upkeep needed on paintwork, the garden, etc. However, houses inevitably fall into disrepair eventually, and the time or money needed to repair or renovate a property might be just that factor that is making the current owners sell. If you're considering buying an older property, you'll need to be aware of the kind of things that could be wrong with it. It's worth getting a good idea of why the present owners are moving; if the house, or a major room, has very recently been redecorated, this could be an indication that certain problems, such as large subsidence cracks, are being disguised. Any such house will need a very thorough survey from a vigilant surveyor.

Damp, rot, structural problems and infestation (eg, of woodworm) are the major problems to worry about when buying an older property. Not only do these difficulties cost a great deal to remedy, but while they exist they seriously undermine the structure – and the value – of the house. Other somewhat less serious problems can include such things as uneven floors, roofs that need retiling (or rethatching) tree roots that are threatening the foundations of the house, blocked drains, etc. All of these difficulties are expensive, and extremely inconvenient, to remedy.

Less drastic, but still inconvenient, problems include such things as paintwork in poor condition, irregularly-shaped rooms, plasterwork that needs renewing, ingrained dirt from cigarettes, solid fuel, and the general patina that is left by years of occupation. For the enthusiast these can be challenges that make him or her itch to start work; for busy or poorly-off people, or those with several young children around, such houses sound more like nightmares than the dwellings of their dreams. If you are considering buying an older house, take these factors into consideration when you are estimating how much you are prepared to pay for the property, and don't underestimate the expense of putting the problems right; tasks such as reroofing, replacing damp courses, relaying floors, treating woodworm, etc, can very easily cost thousands rather than hundreds of pounds.

Aesthetics
If you are going to buy an older house, it is almost inevitable that you will want to change the decor to suit your own taste. These alterations may be very small, for instance simply changing the colour of the paintwork, or they may be quite major – even to the extent of knocking two rooms into one, or building an extension. There are often situations where the facilities are perfectly adequate functionally, but leave a great deal to be desired aesthetically. This is particularly true of all aspects of plumbing – kitchens, bathrooms, toilets, and the pipes themselves – where the antiquated equipment and installation grates on the modern preference for flat, hygienic, wipe-clean surfaces. Heating systems too may be inconvenient, inefficient or uneconomical, especially if they were installed in the days when fuel was much less expensive than it is nowadays.

Security
Many older houses are ill-equipped to keep unwanted visitors at bay; these days we are more security-conscious, partly through necessity as the incidence of theft, burglary, vandalism and assault has risen. In older houses items such as door locks, window catches, outside lighting, etc, may be hopelessly inadequate for good security, so you will need to consider the cost of making the house reasonably secure.

Amenities
Some older houses are lacking in what could be described as basic amenities – a washbasin, an inside toilet, a fixed bath, adequate natural light, etc. In these instances you may be able to obtain a grant to help you improve the house's facilities (see the next pages), but you will have to pay for part of the work yourself, and put up with the inconvenience. Other problems that might need working on are the plumbing, the wiring, and heat insulation (such as lagging of water pipes and water tank, loft insulation, double glazing, draught-proofing windows and doors, etc). Once again, grants may be available towards the cost of the work.

The cost of all the above must be considered when you are making an offer for an older house you are interested in – remember, too, to take into account whether the house needs urgent redecoration work; for instance, if pebbledashing or weatherboarding needs replacing, or if a fitted carpet is badly stained or soiled.

Renovating older property

You may have decided, or are thinking seriously about the possibility, of taking on an older property that needs work done to it. The first thing to decide is how much work you are able to take on yourself, or with your household or friends, and how much needs to be done by professionals. As well as taking your skills into consideration, this decision also needs to be based on how much time you can spare for the renovation work, also how long a time you are prepared to spread the work over.

Improving a property is an excellent task for DIY enthusiasts, but can become a millstone round the neck of anyone who doesn't really know just how much work is involved. The amount that you can take on yourself will be limited by your skills; for instance, you may be happy doing painting, carpentry, erecting plasterboard, putting in a new bathroom suite, even relaying floorboards. Some jobs, such as plastering, fitting central heating, glazing, bricklaying, etc, need training; you might have these skills yourself, but if not you will need to call in outside help. Some jobs, such as rewiring, fitting gas appliances, altering staircases or levels of floors or ceilings, treating damp or woodworm, re-roofing, etc, all need qualified professionals. Don't be tempted to let enthusiastic amateurs do the work for a lower price; as well as being potentially dangerous, it's not worth tying up a great deal of money in a job that might prove totally unsatisfactory.

Permission

Remember that you may well require planning permission for radical changes; make sure that you don't agree to buy a property for improvement before you have obtained outline planning permission. For more minor work you may not require planning permission, but still may need approval under building regulations. If you want to make a new access for vehicles to your property you may find that you require planning permission. Planning permission is discretionary – ie, even if there is nothing palpably wrong with your proposed scheme it may still be turned down. Approval under building regulations is not discretionary; if your proposed scheme meets the regulations, approval must be given. If you are doing any drastic structural alteration, you will require the services of a qualified architect or chartered surveyor. Do check, too, that your property is not under any restrictive covenants, which are surprisingly common. Listed buildings will also have aesthetic and structural restrictions on what can be done to them.

Grants
Local council grants are available to help defray the costs of a variety of basic improvements to older properties. First of all you may find that your council operates a scheme for rehabilitating old properties; you buy at a very low rate and the council gives grants towards the cost of renovation. Financing a property that requires substantial improvement can be difficult; some building societies will lend only a portion (say 70%) of the sum required, some will only lend after the improvements have been made (so that you will require a bridging loan to cover the intervening time), and others will not lend money on older properties at all. Check the financial position very carefully before you take on a property for renovation, and obtain exact details of the grants you will be entitled to.

Grants from the local council will not cover the total cost of the intended improvements; you will, as a rough and ready guide, pay about half of the cost, so include these sums in your calculations over a buying price. Statutory council grants are available for fitting basic amenities to your property, for instance a fixed bath or shower, a sink, hot and cold water, an inside toilet. If the property requires extra work to make these things possible (for instance the building of a bathroom, or the bringing of mains water to the property), the grant may be extended to help towards this work as well.

Discretionary council grants may be available to bring your property up to acceptable standards, even when it is already fitted with the basic requirements. The guidelines are to ensure that, when the work is done, the property will have the following:

- Freedom from damp
- Adequate natural light and ventilation
- Adequate and safe electrical lighting and wiring
- Adequate drainage
- Structural stability
- Satisfactory arrangement of rooms
- Satisfactory facilities for preparing and cooking food
- Adequate heating facilities
- Adequate storage for fuel and refuse
- Adequate insulation.

Extra grants may also be available to help towards adapting a house for a handicapped person, installing medical equipment such as a kidney machine, etc. Your local council offices will have full details of all grants available.

SECTION THREE

FINDING WHAT YOU WANT

By now you are sure you want to move and have set parameters for the area you are prepared to consider and the ideal type of accommodation. You might be champing at the bit to start looking, but the trouble you have taken already to decide exactly what you want will have saved you time on this next stage.

You're now beginning to move on from the general to the specific; seeing how close to your ideal home you can get. There are various ways of going about seeing and choosing what you want, but first if possible it's advisable to have a drive around the chosen area. There are a number of things to keep a look out for as you go. Obviously you will quickly notice if there are any particular roads or streets you especially like – or dislike! Take a local street map with you and underline the names of roads you are particularly attracted by, and put a cross through those you are definitely not prepared to consider. Even though you have generally studied the amenities and the size of your chosen town, taking a good look around puts it all into perspective. In the long run you will save yourself time by doing this; when you are inundated by house particulars from estate agents, local papers and magazines you'll be able to discard some quickly or rank others with high priority as you recognise the street name or district.

You'll also quickly find yourself noticing the 'For Sale' signboards of the local estate agents. You'll soon come to see which of the agents seem most popular with sellers, and this will help you to select the estate agents to visit first for particulars. The distribution of boards in a location may give you a few clues to the area you're looking at, or hint at a possible problem. For example, if you notice a road with a great many 'For Sale' signs you might find that there are plans for road-widening or changes in traffic flow, which could mean increased noise (and inconvenience) from fast traffic and building machinery in the future. Or possibly industry is moving into the area, spoiling the views or producing unpleasant smoke or gases. Perhaps other environmental changes are looming which are causing several people to want to sell quickly; you may even discover that there is a compulsory purchase order on the house itself, and that you would have to sell up within months.

Not all areas where you see clusters of sale boards together are problem areas, of course. Some locations seem to have a constant turnover of houses as people move on to other types of property. Estates of small, new houses or flats that are ideal for first-time buyers will see a rapid turnover as the buyers feel they can move on to something bigger. Relatively new estates of terraced or semi-detached houses on the outskirts of towns or villages will also often have a 'passing through' population; occupants will move on as their family size increases, or as they become able to afford houses with more character, more space, or ones closer to the centre of town. And, in contrast, few signboards could mean that the residents on that estate are very happy with their homes and see few reasons to move, or it could mean that houses in that location are very slow to sell. Once you have been looking for a little while you'll become quite a good judge of whether an area is popular or unpopular – and the reasons why!

Other things to look out for include any derelict properties nearby which may soon be knocked down and replaced by flats. Alternatively, they may be inhabited by squatters, who might not make very congenial neighbours. Have a look at the whole tone of the neighbourhood: are there any signs of vandalism, such as broken windows, graffiti, telephone boxes out of order? Are there any pubs, clubs, social halls, etc, nearby, which may produce loud music or rowdy behaviour when you're trying to sleep? Do people generally keep their houses and gardens in good order and attractive, or does the whole location look rather run down?

All in all your drive around will give you useful information and a 'feel' for the place. Take a notepad with you to jot down first impressions or questions to ask at a later date. If you already know that you are interested in particular roads, go round again and mark on your local map where such things as bus-stops, postboxes, one way streets, etc, are. Don't try to be too detailed at this stage; you'll have plenty of opportunity for further sightseeing and checking as your hunt goes on.

Checklist for choice of road/locality

Are there any roads or localities I'm particularly interested in? If so, which ones?	Are there any roads or localities I'm definitely not interested in, no matter how tempting the property prices? If so, which ones?
....	....
....	....
....	....
....	....
....	....

Using an estate agent

Before you decided to move you probably rarely noticed the variety and number of 'For Sale' signboards outside houses, flats and offices throughout the country. Once you start looking for property yourself, you'll spot boards up to half a mile away! Whatever their general shape, colour or design they are unmistakable, and their relative appeal and style – and even state of repair – can give you a good impression of the different agents in the locality.

Using an estate agent is the most common way of finding a home. Estate agents provide an efficient and usually friendly service, and are aware of all aspects of buying and selling procedures. However, it's important to note a few points about their reason for existence. First and foremost an estate agent is a professional business; it aims to give a good service and maintain a good reputation so that it can make maximum profit. Moreover, as a buyer you have to realise that the estate agent is employed by the owner of the property being sold. The firm's fee is dependent on the sale of a property, for which the estate agent is paid a percentage. Therefore it is in his interest to persuade you to buy. Obviously an estate agent should not give you dishonest information or apply improper pressure to make you buy, nor will a sensible agent encourage you to buy something which is eminently unsuitable; his reputation will only be harmed by doing this. Nevertheless, you must remember that they are not there simply as an impartial free service and friendly advice bureau for you, the buyer; they are in the business to sell houses!

The agent in effect is a broker who brings buyer and seller together. You have no obligation, legal or otherwise, to buy from any firm, and the agents have no duty to you other than the standard prerequisites of the Trades Descriptions Act. Therefore when you first enter an estate agent's office, and find very helpful people who show you a number of properties, possibly give you a cup of coffee and a free map of the area, and then drive you to view a property in the firm's car, remember that this is their job. Don't feel that you can't go to another agent as the first one has

been so nice to you; visit as many estate agents as you want to if they have suitable properties in the right area and in your chosen price range. Estate agents will expect you to shop around, and you will be getting the best range of available properties. Some properties may well be on the books of several agents, but others will be advertised by only one, so it's worth visiting all the agents who deal in property in your chosen locality.

What to expect

You will have been attracted to a particular estate agent by seeing the company name on a signboard or other advertising, or if your eye has been caught by property descriptions in the agent's window. Before you go in make sure that you've sorted out the general type of property you have in mind and the price range you can afford; these are the main points the agent needs to know to give you suitable property particulars. Although by this stage you will have all sorts of specific criteria for your ideal house, by and large these will be irrelevant to the agent. It is a fact that a high percentage of buyers who present a very detailed description of what they want buy something bearing little resemblance to their original idea. As agents know this they will present you with a number of detailed house descriptions, many of which you will feel are totally unsuitable. Nevertheless, it's worth having a glance through all the alternatives; you may come across something fresh that sets you rethinking.

If you are in the area for a few hours and one or two properties have caught your eye, the agent can usually quickly fix up a visit on the spot. Sometimes a member of staff will take you round a property; otherwise you will be given directions and, if the property is unoccupied, a key. Normally a key is only given if the property is unfurnished at the time. Even if none of the houses offered seem on paper to match your ideal, it's well worth viewing a sample property or two just to get used to what to look for and to see inside houses or flats of the type you are interested in. Once again, viewing doesn't put you under any obligation; few people buy the first place they see.

Describing property/alternatives

Property descriptions can be an art form in themselves! The Trades Descriptions Act means that there should be no knowingly false information, but this doesn't rule out the fanciful. The property information sheets you'll be given in profusion contain two types of information. The first type is factual: type of accommodation (for instance terraced, bungalow, flat, semi-detached), number of rooms, room dimensions, special features such as double glazing or central heating, outbuildings, garden, etc. These details should all be as correct as the estate agent can make them, although occasionally they may be relying on information supplied by the present owner. Factual information will also include rateable value and sale price.

The remaining details are sales talk, descriptive passages mainly flattering the property. There is an estate agents' language of exaggeration and unspoken implication which can be quite amusing once you get the hang of it, though it varies from agent to agent in exact detail. No house is described as 'average' or 'unimpressive' or 'immaculate'. 'Ideal for DIY enthusiast' implies that the house requires a lot of work before it will be properly habitable; a 'mature residence' may be a characterless building not quite old enough to be classed as 'period', and not in good enough condition to be classed as 'modernised'. Your idea of a large garden might not be the writer's; his 'small garden' or 'compact patio' may be your idea of 'not-enough-space-for-a-potplant'. 'Must be viewed' suggests that the outside is dull but the inside is more inspiring. 'Living room newly decorated' implies that the rest of the house isn't; 'scope for modernisation' generally means 'desperately needs modernisation'.

Do be aware too that room dimensions can also be misleading, not always deliberately. Older houses are not generally full of easy-to-measure rectangular rooms, and measurements of irregular-shaped rooms need to be simplified for the agent's details. Bay windows also complicate matters, and so do built-in wardrobes, alcoves, larders and so on. Some helpful estate agents will indicate these variations by terms such as '16ft × 13ft (maximum)', or '14ft × 23ft (into window bay)'. You will realise too as you visit that a double bedroom sometimes only means space for the bed and little else; also a study is frequently a room too small to be called a bedroom, rather than the place for storing your desk, typewriter, word processor, computer, filing cabinets and library of 1000 books. On some modern estates all houses may have garages... but they may be all together in a block a few hundred yards away, which is not so funny on a rainy November evening.

Examples from home details are endless, but you will soon become used to seeing through the hyperbole. Take them all with a pinch of salt, and try not to get frustrated or annoyed. After all, you will be selling yourself one day, and you'll want your home to be seen in the best light.

Other methods of finding property

An estate agent is only one way of finding a property; others can be used as well as or instead of hunting via estate agents.

You'll have had a look through some publications early on in your house-hunting to see what prices are like from area to area and property to property. Local newspapers and free advertising broadsheets often have a selection of properties for sale through estate agents, but there are also national and regional periodicals which offer property for sale. The most useful ones are *Dalton's Weekly* and *Exchange and Mart* and, for London and the Home Counties, *The London Weekly Advertiser*. Magazines such as *Country Life* and some of the quality newspapers tend to feature high-quality properties.

In some instances you can by-pass the estate agent and get in direct contact with the seller; in this case the seller avoids the agent's fee and therefore you might be able to push his asking price down a little. You may see a hand-painted 'For Sale' sign outside houses as you drive around, or you may find a property advertised privately in the local press.

Some houses are sold at auction – mainly older, period houses, and large properties with a few acres of land or perhaps a farm attached. If you succeed with your bid, whether with a sealed bid or on the open market, you have a binding contract and have to pay a 10% deposit immediately. As you will forfeit this deposit if you later withdraw, it's advisable to have the house surveyed and thoroughly checked beforehand. On rare occasions people have made personal approaches or written to the owners of a house they particularly like to see if they will sell, but most often this is a route taken by property speculators with old houses on large plots for development into new housing.

One other major method of buying that is becoming more common is buying through building firms. On new estates large companies put up a show house and display plans of the properties to be built; these can then be sold at any stage of development.

Viewing the property

You've worked out your mental picture of your ideal home, and you've received particulars of a property for sale. The time has now come to start finding out how close you can get to your ideal. It's rare to find that the first property you visit is suitable, but even if you baulk on your first glance at the outside don't stop there; it's good practice to view thoroughly inside and outside, to get used to spotting and analysing good and bad points. We'll concentrate first of all on general impressions concerning the property's appearance, facilities and practical details.

Using your senses

You need to use all your senses, not just your sight. Even as you approach the house you should be using your senses of smell and hearing: is the air fresh or stale, or are you near a brewery or farm or waste processing plant? Is there a lot of traffic noise; if so, is the traffic slow-moving, or does it thunder noisily past or involve much crunching gear changes? If you hear an ambulance or fire engine, is this an isolated incident or is there a hospital or fire station nearby? What about aircraft noise or school playgrounds? Noises vary at different times of the day, so think up some questions to find out other sources that could be irritating. If the house is terraced or semi-detached you'll need to know whether the neighbours are quiet or noisy, and how well the walls are sound-proofed; if you're looking at a flat, you'll need to know whether you can hear the households above and below you. Prevailing winds can alter smells; if once a month or so you can just detect a faint smell from the nearby farm it probably won't be a problem, but if this is the exception rather than the rule you may want to think again.

Obviously sight is important too, and your first view will tell you a great deal. Already the particulars will have said if the property has a 'favourable east/west aspect', but you might find that a gasometer blocks out the sunlight, or that a 12ft hedge allows light in only upstairs. You will get an immediate impression of how well looked after the place has been by the state of the garden, if any, and the condition of the windows and front door. Remember, you're not trying to be comprehensive on a first view; if you are tempted to buy you will have follow-up visits, more questions to ask, and finally a survey.

It's worth remembering too that your impressions can be influenced by the time of day and season of your visit. On a glorious summer's day even the most dingy place can appear light; conversely on a gloomy, rainy winter's afternoon you might not feel at your most positive about a property. Think about how the weather might affect the property; is it on low-lying marshy ground that might be liable to flooding? How easy will access be in the snow? Noise may not vary much season by season – although it's worth finding out whether the locality is popular with tourists, foreign students, etc – but it may well vary hour by hour. Neighbours may work shifts and go out or come in at unsociable hours, or may be fond of late-night parties; traffic may increase to unacceptable levels at rush hour; schoolchildren may overrun your open-plan garden at the end of the afternoon, or the man in the flat above may be deaf and have his television blaring all evening. All these matters can be sorted out in detail later if you are interested in the property; it's useful to arrange to visit at a variety of times of day if you are seriously considering buying. On the other hand, if your first glances at the house tell you that you couldn't be happy there, details like this aren't worth pursuing.

General impressions

As you enter you need to be aware of the general overall size, layout and atmosphere of the building. You will find viewing quite different from simply reading the dimensions and number of rooms on the estate agent's particulars. Not all 12ft × 12ft rooms look the same; ceiling heights vary, and the positioning of doors and windows makes a great difference. Lighting and heating elements alter the look, as do built-in shelves or wardrobes, bookcases, windowsills and different-sized windows.

Try to picture yourself or your family living there, and imagine where your furniture would fit – or even whether it would fit. Look out for practical matters of moving from room to room: how many doors need to be opened to get food from the kitchen to the dining table? Is there a serving hatch, or could one be put in? Are there lots of small changes in level; these are quaint at first, but guaranteed to trip up your boss, best friend or toddler eventually. Is the stairway too narrow for furniture to be moved up it easily? Is it a long way from the bedroom to the toilet on a cold winter's night? Can you fit your washing machine or freezer in? Is there enough storage space? Once you picture living there with your own belongings many more common-sense questions will come to mind.

Further investigations

Of course some aspects of the house's appearance can be changed by different decor, and you'll need to be aware of what cosmetic changes you will need, or wish, to make if you buy this particular property. Do you like the wallpaper or paint, the general decor, the carpets? Will your furniture fit in not only physically but aesthetically? If you find a period cottage and have only Habitat furniture, will the two go together? Views out from the inside are important: are they good, bad, or indifferent? Do you overlook field, garages, a garden, a back lane, or other people's houses? This is particularly important regarding rooms where you will spend a great deal of time, whether the living room, kitchen, study or workroom.

Security and privacy are important considerations. How much do you mind being overlooked? Is the garden screened, fenced, or open-plan? You can also bear in mind how security-conscious the owner has been with locks on doors and windows, and possibly a burglar alarm. If there is a garden, how much hidden access is there to back or front door or windows? Are there secluded alleys down the sides of the house, where a burglar could take his time, or are all sides of the house within view of other houses or passers-by?

What to ask the seller

You can only rely so far on observation, particularly in the 15–30 mintues that you generally have to look around a property the first time. Other information has to be gathered by questioning the owner (or, failing that, his or her estate agent). You will want to ask for specific details on what is included in the sale price under the category of fixtures and fittings; are carpets, curtains, lampshades, cooker, venetian blinds, louvre doors, fitted bookshelves, etc, staying? Are all the plants remaining in the garden? What about the greenhouse, or the garden shed? Will the piles of rubbish in the garden, the garage, or the loft be cleared up before the present owners move? If something obviously needs mending, for instance a window or a fence, will it be done before the sale, at the present owner's expense? It's best to ask about any specific item you require or are interested in, and keep a careful note of exactly what is staying, what is going, and what might stay at a price (and if so, what price exactly?).

After this you can check on environmental matters. What are the neighbours and the local shops like? Where are doctors, dentists, post offices? What is parking like for you and for visitors? How helpful are the dustmen? Then you may want to ask questions specific to you or your lifestyle: what about churches, bus routes, trains, schools, adult education centres, cinemas, nightclubs? Who is your MP, and what is the local council like? You want a general picture to help you see just how suitable, or otherwise, this particular property is to you or your family's personalities, likings and lifestyles.

Recording your impressions

Make a photocopy of this list for each property you visit, and write down details as you go around the house.

Property being visited

....

Date and time of visit ....

	Good	Average	Bad
General impression from the outside			
General impression of the inside			
Noise?			
Condition of woodwork, windows, etc.			
Decorative order			

	Yes	No
Are the carpets and curtains included in the price?		

What other fixtures and fittings are staying, or could be bought separately?

....

....

Other details particularly relevant to your household, eg, storage space, rooms for hobbies, garden, etc.

....

....

Running costs

If you have had a good first look round and are quite keen on a property then you will need some idea of the hidden costs of running the place year in, year out. You need to remember that the mortgage payments are only part of the story; annual and quarterly bills will be coming through the new letterbox, sometimes at a terrifying rate! Make sure that you don't take out a mortgage at the absolute limit of your income and then find that you have nothing left for the extra bills that have to be paid on top. You might find it helpful to compare the running costs with any payments you are making where you now live; if you have been living with your family, or lodging, you may find that you haven't been paying a fully realistic sum towards heating, lighting, rates, etc, so be prepared for quite a shock when you take over your own property.

General rates

Rateable value and the level of rates payable should be mentioned on the house particulars. Rateable value is a rough assessment of the amenities offered by the house, for instance how many rooms it has, what accommodation it offers, etc. The rates payable are set by the local council, and are in proportion to the rateable value of the house. Levels of rates will vary from council to council, and are expressed in an amount payable per pound sterling of rateable value. Sometimes this will be less than £1 per £1 of rateable value, for instance the sum might be 60p in the £. In other areas the rates payable may be over £2 or £3 per £, for instance £2.40 per £ of rateable value. Properties of the same type can command very different rates depending on where in the country they are situated, how fashionable the area is, and even the political allegiance of the local council.

It's worth comparing rates on houses of the same type in different sections of the areas you are looking in to see if there is any significant variation. You might find that you could qualify for rent rebates, particularly if you have a low income or are severely disabled, but in general rebates are not easy to come by.

Water rates

Water rates are charged for providing water and for sewage disposal. This rate is related to your general rateable value rather than any metering of water use, and again is set by the local council. Water rate bills, as with general rates, can be paid in a variety of ways – for instance annually, bi-annually, etc – in order to help you plan your payments.

Insurance
The organisation which provides your mortgage will insist that you insure your home against damage to the structure; this is usually arranged by them and can be paid monthly or in a single payment (see **SECTION FOUR: FINANCING YOUR PURCHASE**).

Fuel bills
These costs can vary a great deal, and depend on the time of year, your own lifestyle, the type and condition of the property, and the type of fuel used. You will get a general idea of what to expect from a particular property by asking the seller what his yearly costs have been. Basic costs are for gas, electricity, oil and/or coal. These of course will rise and fall as a reflection of the weather, so note whether you are given figures for a cold year, an average one, or an especially warm one. Central heating will put up bills considerably, but so will heating by individual fires, fan heaters, etc, especially if the property has large rooms or poor draughtproofing. If you have lots of electrically-powered equipment such as a freezer, washing machine, spin dryer, food processor, fan-heaters, TVs, video, stereo, etc, then you can expect a reasonably high electric bill. Remember too that in properties that use both gas and electricity you will have to pay a minimum standing charge for each service every quarter.

Property being visited

....

Rateable value .... **Present level of rates in the £** ....

Annual Costs	
General rates	
Water rates	
Insurance	
Gas	
Electricity	
Coal	
Oil	
Total annual costs	

External structural state

First impressions can be a useful, valid guide to whether a property will suit you or not. Your instincts will probably tell you quickly whether a property is worth only a quick look or a longer one. Space, shape and decorative order of rooms, layout of the interior, fixtures, heating, double glazing and so on are all good pointers to whether you'll find a property pleasant and practical to live in. As well as these factors you will also have to be aware of the structure and fabric of a property; however nice and attractive you find a place, if it's about to fall down or give you huge repair or extension bills it may not really be worth pursuing. So, as you view, be aware of all these general impressions regarding the structure.

Actual structural state is not so straightforward to determine on a superficial look, but there are some obvious signs to watch out for as you wander around the outside and the inside. By and large, the older the property the more likely you are to see outward signs of diseases such as damp, decay, infestation, etc – though a sensible owner will have fought and cured the illness before it became a terminal case. Newer properties are not necessarily entirely free from problems, either when you see the house or in the future, but an NHBC certificate will give you some reassurance if the property has one. You will need to be aware that some of the signs of problems in the structure can take several years to become apparent in visible signs on the walls, floors, timbers, etc; just because you can't see anything doesn't mean that there are no problems.

On a positive note you will more often than not find few major problems. Your first viewing is not meant to be comprehensive; if you want to go further and think about buying a property, you can commission a report from a qualified surveyor and will probably also want a longer, more detailed look round yourself than seems polite on a first visit. Don't be daunted by the number of details that it seems important to notice; after your first few visits to properties on the market you will get used to summing up the details you see, and will probably develop your own personal shorthand to help you fix the details of each property in your mind. Soon your senses and instincts will be weighing up the pros and cons of a particular property almost automatically, and you will find yourself taking in a great deal on a cursory glance at the outside and succinctly summing up the facilities inside. Don't panic if you don't get the chance to look at every detail; you should be able to look at the property as many times as you need to, to satisfy your mind on any particulars.

Don't be in a rush to get inside the property; use your eyes well as you approach it, and get a good view across from the other side of the road if possible before approaching closer. If there are any alleys or roads that give you a view of the back or the side of the property, wander down these and see what you can see; this is often the best way of getting a good look at the external state of the roof. As you're considering practical suitability, you can also be taking in impressions of the structural state; does the property look as though it's in good condition? How does it look in comparison to its neighbours – well cared for, shoddy, or about average? Have lots of the neighbouring properties had to have their windows or doors replaced.

The outside of the property may give you a good impression of the present owner's general attitude towards care and upkeep. If it seems as though repairs have been carried out in a slapdash manner – or not at all – you may find that the inside of the property reflects this attitude too. If the outside is immaculate, you'll probably find that the inside too is in excellent condition.

As you look at the outside of the property check whether there are any major cracks or stains, or signs of decay, on the woodwork or brickwork. A very serious defect is any form of subsidence, or its opposite, heave; these problems usually show up in the form of cracks and are conditions to stay well clear of unless you are prepared for some hefty bills. Major discolorations around the base of the property could be signs of a damp problem; ones further up may be evidence of poor guttering. Glance at the gutters to see what type they are and whether they are in good condition, and have a look at the drainage sites to check that they are clear; if there are signs of flooding nearby the drains may be prone to blockages. Check the condition of what you can see of the roof; do the tiles, slates, thatch, etc, seem even, undamaged, and firmly attached? Does the chimney-stack look stable? Is there much overgrowing with moss or creepers, which might undermine the structure?

Finally, take a general look around the garden. Are there large trees near the property that might block up the gutters with leaves or, more seriously, undermine the foundations with their roots? Is there evidence in the trees and shrubs of a strong prevailing wind? And, what condition are any outhouses in? All these preliminary looks will prepare you for a more detailed look inside.

Internal structural state

Now you have rung the bell or turned the key in the lock (does the bell work properly, is the door in good condition and well fitted, does the letterbox rattle . . . ?!) and had your first look around accompanied by the owner or the agent. You'll now want to ask whether you can look around on your own for a short while; at this stage, having got a general impression of the property, you can concentrate more on structure.

As with the outside of the property, if there is evidence of patching up or making do rather than proper repair work, be alert for signs of problems. If all of the property is tatty except one room which has been newly painted or plastered, this may well be a sign that some cosmetic work has been done over structural problems before putting the property on the market. Don't be too alarmed by hairline cracks in plasterwork; most properties exhibit these, as the plaster tends to crack as it dries out. These aren't serious, though they may warrant some redecoration. Large, or floor-to-ceiling cracks, or those which may hint at stress in the underlying wall, require greater consideration; they are more likely to be evidence of subsidence or heave. Don't be embarrassed to see if the owner can shed any light on the cause of a particular crack.

A general point worth mentioning here is that you should, if you think you are seriously interested in a property, check with the present owners what building work has been carried out recently, and ask to see any major bills. If there is nothing to hide the owner shouldn't object; you would want to know about garage bills if you bought a car, and a property is a much bigger investment.

Take a cursory look at both the wiring and the plumbing. Few properties these days have round-pin plugs, but some still have light sockets hanging from the old cloth-covered twisted wires. If this is the case, be prepared for rewiring in the near future to meet with modern safety standards. Look at the fusebox, and ask whether all the outlets are on a single system (undesirable) or more than one. Check piping to see whether old lead pipes are present or if copper and plastic are used; check for any major signs of leakage or deterioration. Look particularly under the kitchen sink, the toilet and washbasin, around the washing machine and boiler, and at the bottom of the airing cupboard. If possible check that the boiler or water heater – electric or gas – is working properly and efficiently, and check whether the toilet flushes well. Turn taps on and off to see if the movement is easy and efficient. If there are small problems such as a leaky tap you can ask the owner whether they will be fixed before selling; if there are any larger problems, once you have got precise details from your surveyor, you can try negotiating a lower price for the property if you will need to pay out to have them fixed. With heating and hot water systems you should check whether there have been any major problems, and whether they are under guarantee or covered by a service contract.

Insulation is important for minimising your fuel bills. Loft insulation should be a minimum of 4 inches deep to be effective – although you may be able to get a grant towards the cost if the current insulation is inadequate. Check if there is cavity wall insulation; if so, what type is it, and is it under guarantee? Double glazing helps cut down draughts; if there is no double glazing, check whether the windows and doors seem to fit snugly. What type are the window frames, and how much maintenance will they require? Wood needs careful maintenance, PVC very little, and aluminium falls somewhere in between. If the windows are in very poor condition, remember that it can be very costly to replace them.

As you walk around you will be aware of whether the property seems musty, damp or well aired. Condensation is not a problem in itself unless it is allowed to linger and seep into surfaces. Feel the walls of the bathroom, which is where condensation can especially build up, and look for stains and discoloration on all walls, particularly at the very top and very bottom. Dry and wet rot in timber tend to be problems affecting older properties. A surveyor (and specialist firms) will be able to check for these problems more efficiently than you will, but if you see fungus on any timbers, bad staining on carpets near the walls, or smell strong damp, musty smells in ordinary rooms, there may well be trouble of this kind. Both wet and dry rot can be expensive to remedy. Another problem affecting timber is woodworm, or other beetles; if you see any signs, check with the owner whether the problem has been dealt with.

As a final question, it's worth asking the present owners why they are moving. If their reasons seem vague, or too hesitant, then the real answer could be 'because I want to sell before I have to pay out on some large bills'!

Structural state checklists

Photocopy these lists and fill in the details for each property you view.

Property viewed

....

External checklist	Good	Average	Bad
General appearance			
Decorative order			
Brickwork			
Guttering: type			
Roof: type			
Drains: sufficient? Any marks of flooding nearby, or smells?			
Windows: type			
Double glazing, full or partial?			
Sheds, garages and outbuildings: type			

	Yes	No
Is an NHBC certificate available?		
Any signs of damp?		
Any cracks in nearby paths, patios, driveways?		
Any large or dangerous trees or plants nearby?		
Any major repair work recently carried out on the outside?		

Internal checklist	Good	Average	Bad
Plasterwork: general condition and appearance Any cracks?			
Woodwork: general condition and appearance			
Plumbing: type			
Heating: types			
Condition of boiler			
Condition of immersion heater			
Water tank			
Inside roof space: general appearance			
Roof insulation: type			

	Yes	No
Any major work needed?		
Recent repairs carried out inside the house		
Any evidence of damp? (eg, stains on wallpaper, musty smells, mould on inside of windows)		
Any recent maintenance carried out on the timbers supporting the roof, insulation, weatherproofing, etc?		

Using a surveyor

Not everyone who buys a property has a survey carried out, and there is no legal obligation to do so. Some people say that they cannot afford a survey; others don't feel that it's necessary. Certainly in some cases where people have saved on having a survey done no major problems have transpired, but there's no doubt that having another person look over your property before you buy it is a great weight off your mind. In newer properties, especially if they have an NHBC certificate, there ought not to be too many risks, as major faults will be covered by the certificate. But if you're buying an older property it really is well worth having it looked over first; there are numerous problems that can be picked up by a trained observer. This is usually the province of the chartered surveyor, but there are other options; some people ask a friend who may be a builder or a properly qualified architect or decorator. It's also possible to ask the opinion of firms specialising in putting right wet and dry rot and woodworm; they can check the property and give you an estimate for any work that might need doing. Most often, though, a surveyor with the qualification FRICS or ARICS is employed.

If you're not sure how to go about finding a surveyor, your solicitor is a good person to ask for advice – or go by personal recommendation from a friend. Don't ask the seller's estate agent as there might be a clash of interests, since the agent is employed by the owner to make the most of the house.

Once you have chosen the individual or firm, pay a visit. Explain how detailed a survey you require and agree on a fee. The fee should depend on the size of the property, the extent of the work, the age and accessibility of the property, and the professional standing of the surveyor. You're not asking for a detailed account of the state of the wallpaper or judgements of the choice of colour of the bathroom suite; you want to know what hidden problems there are and the ultimate cost of putting these problems right. Your main purpose is to make sure that the property you're buying will not quickly fall down around your ears, become unoccupiable, or present you with enormous, unexpected bills. Your surveyor, as well as checking that the building is basically sound, will be looking for cracks, poor roofing, rotting wood, infestations such as rot and beetle, and similar problems. Your surveyor should also notice whether there are any major problems with the plumbing. If you want a really detailed electrical survey done, either you or your surveyor can arrange for an electrical specialist to do a separate check.

What you should end up with is a detailed report pointing out any particular faults, their extent, whether the problems can be put right and, if so, how long this is likely to take and whether repairs are urgently required. It may then be worthwhile checking with a builder what costs might be involved in correcting the problems. If there are significant faults that will require expensive correction then you may feel that you don't want to proceed any further with the sale. If you feel that you would still like that property, get in touch with the seller and ask either if he will have the fault corrected at his own expense before the sale, or if he will consider an appropriate reduction in the asking price to cover the repairs you will need to make. In cases like this paying for a survey can actually save you money. Even if the owner won't allow you any money off the original price don't give up straight away; it may be worth checking with the local authority whether there is any chance of a discretionary improvement or repair grant.

When you get your surveyor's report it could make very depressing reading, seeming as though what looked like your ideal property is full of potential problems. Don't forget though that your surveyor has a legal duty to you; if the information he gives you proves inaccurate, or inadequate, and results in you incurring unforeseen costs, he can be sued. Therefore he will be erring on the side of caution in the report, noting any signs that might, or might not, be signs of future problems. You will need to differentiate serious problems requiring immediate work and/or outlay, and potential small problems or difficulties that might crop up some time in the future. If you need clarification on any point then ask for it. If you want any further investigation you can arrange for the surveyor to go back again and view a specific point, for instance whether repairs will be needed on the roof before the next winter, or arrange for an expert in a particular field, for instance woodworm, to view the property. Remember though that you will need to pay an additional fee for additional information. Your surveyor, or local building firms, may also be able to give advice on any building or extension work you are thinking of having done on the property.

At the end of the day you want to be confident that the property you are buying is in a good structural state and is a sound investment. Of course there will always be repair bills on any property, even a new one, in time; what you want to know though is that you're not going to be faced with massive structural repair bills when you've just paid out for the property itself.

Remembering what you see

As you move from room to room of any property that you are particularly interested in, look out for features that are difficult to pin down from estate agents' particulars. Use these notes as a basic starting point, and jot down anything that will be of particular significance to your household.

Hall/landing			
Is there any place for muddy wellingtons, etc?		**Yes**	**No**
Is the cupboard under the stairs of reasonable size?		**Yes**	**No**
Is there a sizeable airing cupboard?		**Yes**	**No**
Are there sufficient powerpoints?		**Yes**	**No**
Is there easy access to the loft, eg a pull-down ladder?		**Yes**	**No**
How big is the loft?	**Small**	**Medium**	**Large**

Living rooms			
Are the heating units adequate?		**Yes**	**No**
Are there sufficient convenient powerpoints?		**Yes**	**No**
Are the window-ledges at an acceptable level?		**Yes**	**No**
Will your bookshelves, dining table, etc, fit?		**Yes**	**No**
Are the lighting arrangements adequate?		**Yes**	**No**
What size are the windows?	**Small**	**Medium**	**Large**

Kitchen		
Is there plumbing for a washing machine?	**Yes**	**No**
Are the lighting arrangements adequate?	**Yes**	**No**
Are there adequate ventilation facilities?	**Yes**	**No**
Is there room for a freezer, fridge-freezer, tumble drier?	**Yes**	**No**
Is there sufficient worktop/draining board space?	**Yes**	**No**
How many of the cupboards and units are built in?		

Bedrooms		
Are the heating units adequate?	**Yes**	**No**
Are there any built-in cupboards?	**Yes**	**No**
Are there any sloping eaves which eat into the space?	**Yes**	**No**
Are there sufficient powerpoints?	**Yes**	**No**
Will there be room for a double bed/bunk beds/ hobbies?	**Yes**	**No**
Where are the larger bedrooms	**Back**	**Front**

Bathroom/toilet		
Is there a shower attachment?	**Yes**	**No**
Are there adequate ventilation facilities?	**Yes**	**No**
Is there any heating?	**Yes**	**No**
Is there storage space for, shaving foam, shampoo, etc?	**Yes**	**No**
Is there a towel rail?	**Yes**	**No**
Is there a medicine cabinet?	**Yes**	**No**

Any other relevant information

....

....

....

....

....

....

....

....

....

Different types of flats

If you're not yet in the property-owning market, and have not got a great deal of capital behind you, then you could be looking at the prospect of buying a flat or a maisonette rather than a complete freehold property. Rather than renting and having nothing in the end to show for it you might prefer to start paying a building society rather than a landlord! For single working people, especially, the wide variety of flats available these days offer an early chance for property investment and ownership as the first step towards a larger home at a later date. Older people too, who find a large house a strain to maintain, can benefit by moving to more compact accommodation, with people close by in case of emergency.

Purpose-built flats

Flats come in a variety of shapes, styles, sizes and types. In recent years, as pressures upon housing needs have increased, many property developers are erecting purpose-built blocks of flats, often buying up old houses with large gardens, knocking down the original buildings, and putting up 3- or 4-storey blocks. The occupiers have their own self-contained apartment with neat washing and cooking facilities, perhaps with a communal central heating system for the building but their own thermostat control. Rather than having to worry personally about maintenance and outside upkeep of the garden, etc, the occupiers pay an estate manager to deal with these concerns. There might be a residents' association to help keep relations with the manager on good lines, and to try to keep a basic check on expenses.

Purpose-built flats are not a new idea; you can see plenty built in the 1920s and 1930s around London and large towns and resorts. Often flats built in this era are called 'mansions'. Purpose-built flats are a convenient kind of accommodation provided that you are prepared to have other people living above, below, and to either side of you. Noise can be a problem, but if you are living on your own you may find that having other people so close can provide ready company or help in times of difficulty.

Conversions

Sometimes developers decide that, rather than knocking down a spacious old house, they will convert the building into several self-contained flats. This can be a good compromise between a large block of flats and a small house; you aren't sharing your stairwells, and other facilities, with dozens of others, and the architecture may well be much more pleasant. You may have your own front door with private outside access and possibly part of the garden as well. Obviously you have fewer neighbours to cope with, although if you don't get on well with the other people in the building you could find yourself too close for comfort!

Sheltered flats

Some small blocks of flats are built to provide sheltered accommodation for elderly or handicapped people. These schemes allow privacy and independence while also ensuring that all the residents have help nearby if needed. Generally there will be a warden available at all times, and each flat will have a bell or intercom that connects with the warden's flat. There may also be the added advantages of communal games rooms, guest rooms, laundry facilities, and sometimes even restaurants. There will also generally be a communal garden, perhaps also a small garden or balcony for each leaseholder to look after privately.

Leasing

The main point to note with flats and maisonettes is that you will almost certainly buy a lease rather than a complete freehold. This means that you have a number of restrictions placed on you by the freeholder regarding decoration, maintenance, etc. You buy the right to live in the unit for a given number of years; this is generally 99 at the beginning of a new lease; if you buy an older lease there will be fewer years left to run on it. At the end of the years of the lease the property reverts to the person holding the freehold at that time.

The freeholder has the right to make certain decisions to protect his or her property; for instance he or she will insist that maintenance work is regularly carried out, that the building (and possibly garden) are well cared for, and that there is reasonable consistency in the way the leaseholders act (for instance, by not painting their parts of the building in lurid colours.) The freeholder or his representative will draw up a lease that arbitrates on these and several other conditions.

First the lease will set out the length of the letting period, access rights, and exactly what is your boundary within the property – and what areas are common property for all the leaseholders. Read through the lease yourself and get your solicitor to check exactly what you are agreeing on.

Costs of running a flat

Whatever flat you buy you need to be aware of the various hidden costs or extra running costs that will be entailed – these, of course, are in addition to the normal running costs such as gas, electricity, water rates, etc.

Ground rent
Ground rent is a regular payment. It is not a vast amount – perhaps £50–100 per annum – and is payable to the freeholder. Payment of this allows you the right of access to the communal driveway, entrance lobby, lift or stairway, whichever is relevant; in other words, it permits you access to your own front door. In some cases the amount is set at one level for 10–20 years and a clause in the lease writes in a set increase after this time.

Maintenance charges
These can vary a great deal depending on not only the state of the property but also the individual freeholder. Basically the tenants of a property are responsible for paying for the upkeep, or maintenance, of the property. Costs are shared among the different tenants in any one property. Maintenance charges can be a bit of a snare to the unwary, as they don't only mean that you pay for the upkeep or repair of your particular flat or bit of outside wall; even if you own the basement flat you could easily find yourself helping to pay for a new roof, or a complete repainting. It's therefore important to get your solicitor to check early on exactly what obligations your lease lays on you.

It's also important from this point of view to check extra carefully what state the rest of the building is in, not just your proposed flat; your flat may be fine, but if the present tenant is moving out just before a large bill comes in for renewing the damp course or replacing the windows of another flat, you could find yourself having to fork out just when you can least afford it. If you have a surveyor ask him or her to make an assessment of the possible work on the whole block or converted house that might need to be done in the next few years. Check, too, exactly what proportion of maintenance bills you will be required to pay; it may not be as obvious as you think. For instance, if there are two flats in a building, but they are of different sizes, you may find that the charges are split 70 to 30 rather than 50/50. Or there may be other disadvantages built into the lease; for instance you may find that if you have the top flat in a block you are responsible for the state of the roof.

It's not unknown for people attached to a building firm to take on a freehold and then have ready work for their firm when required (or, in the case of unscrupulous firms, when not required!) These firms can be rather over-zealous in carrying out repairs, and are not always cheap.

Management fees

These are paid to the estate manager for his work for supervising work carried out and the general running of the property; fixing insurance (paid, of course, by you) arranging repairs, listening to complaints, etc. This amount, too, can creep up alarmingly if not queried early on. In some situations a sinking fund can be opened by the freeholder whereby you are required to pay large sums in advance towards major repairs to be carried out in one or two years' time; this scheme, of course, means that the freeholder earns the interest on that money rather than you in the meantime.

All in all the influence of the freeholder is very important. By and large freeholders are in the business for business reasons, not philanthropy. Check with tenants other than the ones you are buying off to see what they think of the freeholder; also check maintenance and management charges for the previous few years. With your own house you usually have a choice as to when (or whether) to paint or repair; with a flat you generally don't. Use this list to fill in charges for previous years to help assess your running costs for a particular flat.

Property being visited

....

Ground rent		
Management charges		
Maintenance charges		
Total hidden running costs for a flat		
Are there any arrangements for a sinking fund?	**Yes**	**No**
Does it seem as though any major work will be needed soon?	**Yes**	**No**

SECTION FOUR

FINANCING YOUR PURCHASE

Although there are currently several sorts of financial institution in the mortgage market (see pp. 96–99), building societies and banks are the main lenders, especially to the first-time buyer.

Building Societies

When considering who to approach for a mortgage it's more than likely that your first thoughts will turn towards a building society. There are over 160 different societies in the UK, providing almost 75% of all mortgage finance, so the chances are that a building society is where you'll end your quest for a mortgage. Their source of finance are those of us who have building society savings accounts – there are four such accounts to every mortgage account.

When approaching a building society, it's worth bearing in mind that you'll probably have a better chance of getting a mortgage if you've already saved with them on a fairly regular basis for at least two years. The local manager will have a good idea of the value of the local property market and he will be able to help you decide just how much you can afford on your salary and savings. He will also arrange insurance, home improvement and top up loans, and second mortgages for you.

It can pay to save with more than one society because many building societies have their own rules about the sort of properties they will lend on. For instance, some may not give mortgages on freehold flats, and many won't lend on conversions.

Building society rates are more or less on a par with banks and, in the case of the larger societies, somewhat less competitive. Local, single-branch societies quite often offer a ¼ or ½% less on mortgage interest.

In the mid 1980s, competition to provide mortgage finance really started to hot up and building societies were forced to start aggressive mortgage marketing. As a result, there are all sorts of packages now offered by the societies from mortgage offer certificates to brandish at buyers to complete home purchasing services.

In 1987, the Building Societies Bill is due to become law and this will make fundamental changes to the financial services which building societies can offer their customers. For the first time, societies will be able to manage mortgage investments, finance pension schemes, run their own estate agencies and conveyancing services and the very large societies – those with assets of more than £100 million – will be able to offer unsecured personal loans (as the banks do), for instance bridging loans.

Banks
In the late 1970s and early 1980s the big four banks, Barclays, Lloyds, Midland and Natwest, entered the mortgage market with a lot of funds and fanfare and then quietly withdrew. Now they're back again but this time they look set to stay. Other banks, too, such as the TSB, Royal Bank of Scotland, Bank of Scotland, Clydesdale Bank, Co-operative Bank, Yorkshire Bank, Girobank and many foreign banks are also competing for mortgage business.

The majority of the British banks will usually offer mortgages of up to 95% of the purchase price and the TSB Scotland and the Co-operative Bank will sometimes offer 100% advances. The foreign banks on the whole prefer to deal with the second-time buyer where the risk of defaulters is lower and many of these banks will not consider mortgage applications under £30,000.

High Street banks' interest rate bears favourable comparison to the building societies' because of the way it is calculated. A building society usually calculates the interest you owe on your loan every six or twelve months, whereas the banks calculate on a daily basis which means that the balance reduces daily. For example, a bank which quotes a rate of 11% is offering more or less the same as a building society quoting 10.75%.

There is very little to choose between a bank or building society. You may get a more personal service from a building society but a better rate from a bank. It will depend, in the first instance, on your personal preference.

Banks *v* Building Societies: a comparison of rates (October 1986)
(based on a £25,000 repayment mortgage over 25 years)

Bank/ Building Soc	Interest rate	APR	Net monthly repayment
Midland Bank	11	11.5	177.25
Barclays (constant net)	11	11.6	178.00
Lloyds	11	11.7	178.50
Halifax (deferred)	11	11.9	180.92
National Westminster	11	11.8	180.93
Barclays (annually rev)	11	11.6	188.75
Abbey National	11	11.7	192.00
Nationwide	11	11.9	192.03

Counting the cost

The most important initial step you have to take once you've decided that you want to buy your own home or move to a new one, is to calculate how much you can afford. This sum doesn't just take into account the price of the property itself, it has to include a (long) list of incidental costs. Too many people come to grief by under-estimating moving and running costs. These will vary according to whether you are buying for the first time, or selling one home and buying another.

In later pages, we'll go into greater detail about the individual costs, but as an initial guide these are the services for which you will have to pay:

First time buyers

- Solicitor's conveyancing fees (approximately ½–1% of purchase price)
- Stamp duty (on properties over £30,000 at start of 1987)
- Land registry fee
- Search fees
- Survey fee (this varies from about £150 upwards)
- Lender's valuation fee
- Mortgage arrangement fee
- Removal van/firm costs
- Buildings insurance

As a rough rule of thumb these costs approximate to 5% of the purchase price and don't include any new furniture or fixtures and fittings you might have to buy.

Second time buyers

As above, plus

- Estate agent's fee
- Higher fee to solicitor for conveyancing on two properties (about 2%)

As a rough rule of thumb these costs approximate to 10% of the purchase price.

These are all one-time only costs. However, if you want to find out how much you can afford to repay monthly to your lender you must deduct running costs and the cost of living from your monthly income (after tax). The difference will be what you can comfortably afford to pay towards a mortgage.

Running costs and cost of living

If you refer to **SECTION ONE: WHY MOVE** you'll find a checklist to help you arrive at your calculations but here's a reminder of what you must allow for running costs:

- General rates
- Service charge/ground rent
- Gas/electricity/oil/solid fuel
- Water rates (optional hosepipe licence)
- Annual life insurance premium
- House and contents insurance premiums
- Telephone
- General maintenance and redecorating
- Garden (tools, plants, etc)

General rates and water rates vary from town to country, from borough to borough and are priced according to the size of the property. So, once you have decided which area you're moving to and the size of property you are looking for, you can find these costs out from an estate agent or the town hall. The life insurance premium is determined by what sort of mortgage you choose and the requirements of the lender. To find out the other costs, you can either make an educated guess or ask your friends who own similar properties how much it costs them to run their homes.

You should have a fairly accurate idea about your cost of living but here's a reminder:

- Travel (fares; car maintenance, tax, insurance, petrol)
- HP loans (furniture, kitchen appliances, car, stereo, etc)
- Credit cards
- Clothes
- Food
- Regular savings
- Life insurance/pension premiums
- Any other expenditure such as presents, holidays, etc.

Mortgage costs

This, of course, is your single largest expense: the amount you agree to pay monthly to your lender. Having done your sums, you should discuss with your prospective lender the amount you can afford and they are willing to advance (90%, 95%, etc, of the asking price), the type of mortgage which best serves your short or long term interests (repayment, endowment, etc) and the interest rate your lender will charge. Initially you may have to pay anything up to 10% of the purchase price in cash, although in these competitive times, some mortgage companies will advance 100% of the purchase price but this will depend on very specific requirements – an older leasehold property, for instance, would probably not qualify.

Mortgage advances and tax relief

Most lenders will offer mortgages up to 2½–3 times your annual salary. However, if the asking price of a property is equal to 2½ times your gross salary, don't necessarily expect to be offered a 100% mortgage, as this depends on the lender's valuation.

The loan

For a single person on a salary of say £12,000, a mortgage would be calculated on a multiplication basis of 2½–3, in other words, £30,000–36,000. The situation is slightly different for married couples or for two people buying a property together.

For instance, Mr and Mrs Smith have calculated that they need to borrow £50,000 to buy the house of their dreams. Mr Smith earns £14,000 and Mrs Smith £10,000. A typical building society would take into account 2.75 times the main income which, in this instance is Mr Smith's, and 1 × the secondary income, Mrs Smith's. The mortgage offer would therefore be:

£14,000 × 2.75 = £38,500
£10,000 × 1 = £10,000
Total = £48,500

Having allocated their savings towards solicitor's fees, etc, the Smith's are still short of £1,500. They might be able to make this up with a top up loan or by shopping around various lenders, as many of the small building societies offer more competitive mark ups, eg 2.6 × joint salary which would have given the Smith's £62,400.

What you must always remember to take into account is how much you can realistically and sensibly afford.

Gross income, by the way, is regarded by lenders as being basic pay so it doesn't take into account varying commission, bonuses or private income such as investments. Some lenders will include commission if you can produce an employer's certificate which states that you'll continue to receive commission at the same rate (or higher).

Maximum advance as percentage of valuation

This depends on two things: the type of property for which you need the mortgage and the lender's valuation.

Should you ever default on your mortgage, the lender needs to be sure that he can resell the property and recoup all the money he has lent you. So, when you apply for a mortgage, the lender will send his own valuer to see the property and to assess whether it's worth the asking price. Quite often, the lenders' valuation will be less than the sale price. But, as we've mentioned before, in times of competition when property prices are rising strongly, the lender may agree to advance 100% of the sale price.

Although many people consider that older properties were better built than modern ones are, lenders view them as a greater lending risk because of potential dry rot, subsidence and so on, which could cause structural damage and affect the resale price. Other factors which might prevent the lender advancing any more than 90–95% of the sale price include leasehold property – where anything with less than 60 years to run is considered risky – and a freehold flat which some mortgagees refuse to lend on at all.

Length of loan

Usually, the maximum term over which you can repay your mortgage is 25 years and the minimum 10, but some lenders will extend this to 30 years. Normally, too, the term of the loan should end before you retire but many lenders will waive this if the borrower has good pension prospects.

Tax relief

Tax relief, at the rate of tax which you pay, is given on mortgages up to £30,000 (£60,000 for unmarried couples). In 1983 the Mortgage Interest Relief at Source (MIRAS) scheme was introduced. In short, this scheme means that tax relief is taken into account before you make any mortgage repayments. The lender makes the calculations and charges you the net monthly repayment.

For example: Miss Brown has a mortgage of £27,000 with a building society, with interest of 13%. The building society will work out her tax relief – she pays the basic income tax of 29% – as follows:

Payment due before tax relief:	£270.83
Less tax relief at 29%:	£78.54
Miss Brown pays a monthly instalment of:	£192.29

If your mortgage is greater than £30,000, eg £35,000, you'll only get tax relief on the £30,000. If you pay tax at a higher rate than 29%, you're entitled to greater tax relief (but still only on mortgages up to £30,000) but this would have to be claimed through your tax office, as MIRAS only operates at the basic rate of tax.

Bridging loans and home improvement loans normally qualify for tax relief.

Types of mortgage

There are several different types of mortgage available, catering for different financial requirements. No frills, straight repayment mortgages used to be the most common types which people took on but now around half of new borrowers opt for endowment mortgages. Also on offer are pension-linked or unit-linked mortgages, Homeloan schemes and deferred payment mortgages. You should choose the type of mortgage which best suits your financial circumstances.

Repayment mortgage

There are two types of repayment mortgage: the constant net repayment and the deferred or gross profile repayment mortgage.

The constant net repayment mortgage is a capital repayment type of mortgage where you pay back both interest and capital on a monthly basis so that when you reach the end of your repayment term, say 25 years, you will no longer owe anything to the lender. Monthly payments remain constant unless there's a change in interest rates, and you can reduce the amount of the loan at any time by paying a lump sum.

The interest on the first £30,000 qualifies.for tax relief (MIRAS) at the rate of tax which you pay, so most lenders will calculate your monthly payments on a net basis, reclaiming the tax relief from the Inland Revenue. For example, this means that when the interest rate is 11% and you are paying tax at the rate of 29%, you will be charged a net rate of 7.8%.

The amount which you repay each month depends on how much you've borrowed, the length of the term, eg 20 or 25 years, and the current rate of interest. Obviously if you choose a short term in which to repay the mortgage, say 10 years, your monthly repayments will be much higher.

The deferred repayment mortgage would probably suit you if you're a bit squeezed for money now but you're fairly sure of steady increases to your salary in the future. Again, this type repays capital and interest to the lender on a monthly basis but the difference is that you pay off more interest than capital to begin with.

This means that you benefit from greater tax relief at the beginning of your mortgage term and so your monthly payments are significantly smaller than a straightforward, constant net repayment mortgage. However, as the interest element of the loan gets smaller, so does your tax relief and your yearly payments increase. The total amount paid over the whole term of the loan is more than what you would pay for a constant net repayment mortgage. If mortgage interest rates fall, you can if you wish maintain your repayments at your current rate and so reduce the term of your mortgage.

Repayment mortgages are, on the whole, the cheapest but you may be asked to take out a protection policy which would pay off the outstanding loan if you were to die before the end of the mortgage term.

Endowment mortgage

This is an increasingly popular form of mortgage which links a capital loan with an endowment assurance policy. What this means is that you only pay interest to the lender which, of course, is eligible for tax relief, plus a monthly premium to an insurance company. (This doesn't mean that you have to get the mortgage through an insurance company.)

The monthly premium to the insurance company pays for an endowment policy and, when you reach the end of your mortgage term, the policy pays off the capital to your lender and, usually, provides you with a tax-free lump sum as well.

Despite the abolition of tax relief on life assurance premiums in 1984, endowment mortgages remain popular. The extra interest which lenders used to impose on these sort of mortgages has been abolished and, in some cases, they cost the same as repayment mortgages. They have the advantage of paying off anything outstanding on the loan should you die but the disadvantage is that when mortgage interest rates rise you cannot extend the term of the loan but have to pay the higher monthly rate.

There are three sorts of endowment mortgages to choose from: non-profit, with-profits, and low-cost.

The non-profit endowment mortgage is a non-starter unless you're looking for a top-up loan or second mortgage. The reasons for this are that it's more expensive than a net repayment mortgage and only pays off the capital on your loan – there's no extra nest-egg for you at the end of the term!

The with-profits endowment mortgage isn't cheap in the short term but comparatively beneficial in the long. With this sort of policy you pay a bit more but the insurance company provides annual or three-yearly reversionary bonuses which reflect the profits the company has made by investing your premiums. Over the years, depending on the insurance company's investment performance, the bonuses add up to a rather tidy lump sum which is yours at the end of the mortgage term. Over a shorter period, you'd be better off having a separate savings scheme.

Types of mortgage (cont)

The low-cost endowment mortgage is similar to a with-profits type of endowment mortgage in that the policy provides bonuses. The difference is that the insurance company gets out its crystal ball and assumes that at the end of the loan term, the policy will be worth more than the capital repayment. Having made this assumption, they offer a reduced premium. The only catch is that if they're wrong in their forecasting and your policy is worth less than the balance of the loan due, you will have to find the difference. In practice this is highly unlikely so the risk involved is very low and at the end of your mortgage term you should find yourself free of debt and with a cash lump sum as well. Currently the monthly repayments on many low-cost endowment mortgages is no more than those for a conventional repayment mortgage.

Pension mortgage
This is a more expensive method as far as monthly payments are concerned, but nevertheless a useful type of mortgage if you're self-employed or not a member of a company pension scheme. A pension mortgage kills two birds with one stone: it pays off your mortgage and provides a pension.

As with an endowment mortgage, you pay interest only to the lender and premiums to a life assurance company. The interest qualifies for tax relief as do the pension premiums, so it's a very tax-efficient way of buying your home. At the end of the term, the capital loan on your mortgage is paid off and you receive a tax-free lump sum and a pension. The lender will require you to take out enough life insurance cover to pay off the loan in the event of your death.

One drawback, if you don't count the more expensive monthly payments, is that you have to make your retirement coincide with the end of the mortgage term; in other words, a man who is aged 42 and is due to retire at 65 would have to take a pension mortgage over a 23 year term. As with endowment mortgages, you have to increase your payments if interest rates rise.

Unit-linked mortgage
This works in much the same way as a low-cost endowment but it is more flexible and the lump sum at the end of the term can often be larger. You pay off the interest to the lender and the monthly premiums which you pay to the unit trust company are used to buy units in your chosen investment fund(s). There is quite a wide choice of funds, eg property, gilts, etc, but the one usually

recommended is the managed or general fund which is a mix of all the others and therefore somewhat safer than putting all your eggs in one basket. On past performance, unit-linked investment funds have done better than with-profits policies.

The monthly premiums of a unit-linked mortgage are slightly higher than a low-cost endowment but it's only a small price to pay if you want the flexibility which a unit-linked mortgage offers. Most lenders will assume that units grow by 7.5% each year, which would ensure that the mortgage loan was paid off at the end of the term. However, units usually well outperform that figure which means that the mortgage can be paid off earlier. The second way in which this form of mortgage is flexible is that when you sell your home in order to buy a more expensive one, the mortgage can often be extended for the same monthly premium. Banks are willing to accept unit-linked mortgage plans but some building societies are still not prepared to do so.

Homeloan scheme

This is a government scheme to help first-time buyers who want to buy a home below a certain price (set according to regions by the government), and who save with a recognised lender such as a building society, bank or friendly society. For those who just can't find enough finance but who show that they have saved on a regular basis for at least 2 years, this scheme will provide a tax-free cash bonus of up to £110, depending on the amount that's been saved, and, if this is at least £600, a loan of £600. Details are available from banks or building society branches.

Making your mortgage decision

By now you may be feeling a bit confused by the choice of mortgages available to you, so the following comparisons may help you through the maze.

Comparative monthly payments
Comparative monthly payments on a £30,000 mortgage over a period of 25 years, assuming a constant interest rate of 11% for a single person under the age of 35 paying the basic rate of tax.

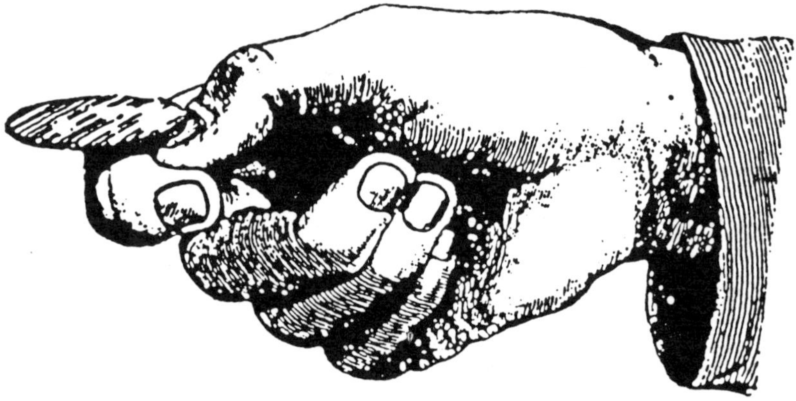

Repayment	Monthly repayment	Protection premium	Total cost (monthly net)
	£230.41	**£7.00**	**£237.41**
Low cost endowment	Monthly interest payments	Endowment premium	Total cost (monthly net)
	£195.25	**£39.40**	**£234.65**
Unit-linked	Monthly interest payments	Unit-linked premium	Total cost (monthly net)
	£195.25	**£42.63**	**£237.88**
Pension linked	Monthly interest payments	Pension premium	Total cost (monthly net)
	£195.25	**£51.10**	**£246.35**

Mortgage criteria

Now that you've made a comparison of costs you should have some idea which sort of mortgage to go for, but to help you here's a checklist of criteria which may guide your decision:

	Constant Repayment	Reduced Repayment	Non-profit Endowment	With-profits Endowment	Low-cost Endowment	Unit-Linked	Pension-Linked
Can I get tax relief on interest	Yes	Yes	Yes	Yes	Yes	Yes	Yes
Can I repay interest and capital	Yes	Yes	Yes	Yes	Yes	Yes	Yes
Can I have my loan paid off at the end of the term and get a lump sum	No	No	No	Yes	Yes	Yes	Yes
Can I vary my payments to suit me	Yes	No	No	No	No	Yes	No
Can I carry forward the mortgage to my next purchase	No	No	Yes	Yes	Yes	Yes	Yes

Protection policies / insurance

If you decide to take on a form of repayment mortgage, your lender will most probably ask you to take out a mortgage protection policy. This is a form of life assurance which pays off what you still owe on your mortgage if you should die before the loan is repaid. However, if you pay off your mortgage before you die, you don't get anything back from the policy.

With endowment, unit-linked and pension mortgages, life insurance is an intrinsic part of the agreement and therefore a mortgage protection policy isn't needed.

Protection policies don't cost very much – the annual premiums are about £2–3 cover for a healthy, non-smoking male for each £10,000 of your loan. They are usually spread over the period of the loan and may decrease as you pay off the loan. Your lender will normally arrange the policy for you at competitive rates. For example:

The Cheshire Building Society has developed a new mortgage protection scheme with NEL Assurance, called Loancare. They say that a man of 28 with a gross monthly mortgage payment of £200 would pay a monthly premium of £3.20, and included in the cover is a benefit which pays the mortgage if the borrower falls ill and is unable to return to work for the remainder of the mortgage term.

Buildings insurance

This is a mandatory requirement for anyone taking out a mortgage on a house because the lender doesn't want to see his security go up in a puff of smoke and, for that matter, nor does the borrower! Most lenders such as banks, building societies and insurance companies will insist on arranging the cover for you but sometimes you can make a case for doing your own shopping around insurance companies for competitive rates. However, the lender will have to approve the policy. If you are buying a flat, buildings insurance won't necessarily be your responsibility unless you also purchase the freehold of the whole property.

Basically, what you are insuring against is the rebuilding costs of your house if it is damaged by fire or flood, and other less common hazards such as lightning, explosion and earthquake. The temptation, of course, is to under insure because the premiums would cost less and the likelihood of your home being damaged is fairly low. Resist the temptation because, if disaster did strike, you might find yourself having to find a lot of money to make up the difference between what your policy provides and the actual costs of rebuilding your home.

For instance, if you are buying a house on a newly-built estate, the builder may quote a lower building price because he has bulk bought his materials and labour. However, if you had to rebuild the house (and it's no longer the developer's responsibility), a local builder's charges will be more expensive for a 'one-off' job. Similarly, you may purchase an older house for a bargain price in an unfashionable area, but the cost of rebuilding it would well exceed the purchase price.

Normally, when your lender has a valuation done of your intended purchase, a rebuilding valuation will be made at the same time, taking into account local rebuilding costs. The lender will then take out a policy for you to cover the costs, a typical premium being about £1.60 to £2 per £1000 insured per annum. Once a year you will receive notification of an automatically updated cover, to keep in line with inflation. This is a figure which reflects labour and materials charges, not the market value of your property.

Contents insurance

This is not a mandatory mortgage requirement, just common sense. For example, buildings insurance won't cover damage to contents and carpets if your water tank flooded. In addition, of course, there is the greater risk of theft, especially if you live in a city. Premiums reflect the area you live in, the more urban your location, the higher the premium. In London, for instance, you can expect to pay up to £90 a year for £10,000 worth of contents.

Usually, you can establish the insurance value of your contents yourself but special items such as jewellery, antiques, paintings, gold, silver and other precious metals will have to be valued separately by a representative of the insurance company. The premium will of necessity be higher. You may already have insured your possessions if you're living in rented accommodation but moving to your own home you will probably purchase extra furniture, furnishings, appliances, etc, so you will need extra insurance and your insurance company will need to know your new address and the age of the property to assess the risk.

Valuation and mortgage survey

Once you've made an offer on a property, the lender whom you've approached for a mortgage will appoint a local surveyor to produce a valuation report (cost approx £60 for a £40,000 purchase). This entails a very basic structural survey and takes into account comparable property prices in the area in order to ensure that the property is not too over-priced, providing adequate security for the loan.

This report is usually for the lender's eyes only but, in many if not most cases, you can arrange with the lender for a more comprehensive home buyer's report (cost approx £145 for a £40,000 purchase). When the lender's surveyor visits the property he will carry out a more detailed survey and will send you and the lender a copy of his report.

If the valuation is satisfactory the lender will send a detailed letter of the loan instructions to your solicitor – you've got your mortgage!

A down-valuation

Quite often the lender's valuation will be what's known as a 'down-valuation'. This means that the property has been valued at less than the asking price, a fairly common occurrence as the lender tends towards a conservative view while the seller and the buyer are more optimistic. If this happens and you don't have the spare cash to make up the difference, you have three options.

1 You go back to the seller and make a lower offer;
2 If the seller won't budge, make up the difference with a top up loan;
3 You withdraw your offer and look for another property.

A retention on your mortgage offer

On an older property, another factor which might influence the lender is the need for certain repairs to the property. For instance, the valuer may state in his report that some roof re-tiling is necessary to stop water seeping through and damaging the timber roof supports, but that once this repair has been carried out the property is, in his opinion, worth the asking price. In this case, the lender might stipulate in his mortgage offer that £1000 is retained from the full mortgage loan until the repairs are carried out. Once the roof has been re-tiled, the lender's valuer would reinspect the property and if the work was satisfactory, the lender would then release the £1000 to you. Again, you are faced with options in this situation:

1 Negotiate with the seller to drop the purchase price by £1000 or pay for the repairs himself.
2 Obtain a bridging loan for £1000 (plus the estimated cost of repairs) to cover the period between completion and the repairs being done.

Full structural survey
This is a sensible precaution for your own peace of mind (cost approx £280 for a £40,000 purchase). Although the lender's survey may pick up the obvious defects of a property such as subsidence and dry rot, a full structural survey will report on wiring, plumbing, the state of walls, floors, windows, etc. He may suggest that certain repairs are vital for your own comfort once you move in which will entail spending more money. You can appoint your own surveyor via estate agents, recommendations from friends, the Royal Institution of Chartered Surveyors (see **Useful addresses** (pp. 188–189), or by asking your lender for the name of the surveyor he appoints to do the valuation. Use this checklist to guide you through the process of valuation and survey.

Lender's valuation

Purchase price	Valuation	If less	✓	Retention	✓
		Lower offer		Lower offer	
		Top up		Bridging loan	
		Start again			

House-buyer's report

Purchase price	Valuation	If less	✓	Retention	✓
		Lower offer		Lower offer	
		Top up		Bridging loan	
		Start again			

Private survey	Main repairs recommended	
Name	1	
....	2	
Address	3	
....	4	
Telephone	Total	
....		

Selling your current property

Apparently one of the most stressful times in your life – second only to divorce – is when you sell one property and buy another. Stories abound about chains, false starts and gazumping but, with careful planning (and probably a small element of luck) the process can go relatively smoothly. So why add to your troubles and take on the sale of your home when there are plenty of estate agents who could do the job for you? In a word: cost. Estate agents' fees can vary between 1½ to 3% of the sale price, so if you are prepared to take on the role of an estate agent you can save yourself a lot of money.

Setting a price

This is a crucial figure because you want to avoid under-pricing, which would deprive you of capital towards your next purchase, or over-pricing which could mean delays while the market catches up with your price. On the other hand, you should inflate the figure slightly to allow room for manoeuvre because a buyer will usually put in a lower offer than the asking price. There are several ways of arriving at the right figure:

- Ask three estate agents to come round and price your property. By asking an estate agent to do this you are not giving him instructions to sell, he just hopes that you will. Some agents charge a fee for valuation, so find out first if this is the case.
- Property columns in local newspapers are often a good pointer to the prices being asked in your area, if not in your road.
- Obtain estate agents' price lists for comparable properties in your area or look at the property details on display in their windows.

Having arrived at your asking price, you should then take into consideration two other factors: the structural state of your property and fixtures and fittings. If there are any repairs which need doing, it's better if you do them before putting the property on the market. A good lick of paint will make your home look more attractive, too. If there are any serious faults which you are not prepared to remedy, then your asking price will have to be lower to make allowances.

When you move you are quite entitled to take fixtures and fittings such as carpets, curtains, kitchen appliances and bookshelves with you. However, you may decide that you want to sell some or all of these items to your buyer. If this is the case, you must decide whether they are included in the sale price and if so add a suitable figure to your sale price.

Promotion
As your property will not be going out to prospective buyers on estate agents' lists, you have to find a means of advertising your sale. Again, there are several ways (or a combination) of doing this:

- Newspaper advertising. For a relatively small outlay, between £15 and £50 depending on lineage, you can insert an advertisement in a local, specialist (eg *Exchange and Mart*), or national newspaper. You should be very careful in deciding what features about your property are most likely to catch a prospective buyer's eye and which will appeal, eg area, large garden, number of bedrooms, central heating, etc. Try not to use too many abbreviations in an attempt to save on the cost of lineage, as they can become hard to understand. Give a daytime telephone number if possible but, if not, make sure that you stipulate an evening number and the time at which you'll be available to answer the 'phone.
- Make your own 'For Sale' board and put it up at the front of the property. If you live in a flat, make sure that you have the agreement of the tenants in the other flats to do this.
- Property shops. For a small fee you can put details and a colour photograph of your property in a property shop window and any potential buyer gets in touch with you direct.

Particulars
If your advertising is successful, you will have a number of prospective buyers coming round to view the property and they will need a copy of particulars to take away with them. These should include details of the location, accurate measurements of each room, passageways, garden(s); fixtures, power points, radiators, freehold or leasehold, price and the local rates.

Having got this far, you should have saved yourself a substantial amount of money. What you now have to do is answer all enquiries, arrange appointments to view, show all the viewers round your property, sort out any rival bids and then negotiate the final price with the buyer you've chosen. Once you accept an offer, take details of the buyer's name, address, mortgage lender and the solicitor's name and address. Then, unless you are doing your own conveyancing, send the details to your solicitor.

Using an estate agent

When buying or selling a home, a far greater percentage of people use the services of an estate agent rather than do the work themselves. There are hundreds of estate agents' offices throughout the UK and, during property booms, a new one seems to spring up every day. Banks, building societies, even large retailers are now offering property selling services. So what do they offer and how much do they cost?

It all depends whether you're buying or selling: if you're only buying a property, the estate agent's services are completely free; if you're selling, the charge can vary from 1 to 2% for a sole agency, and from 2 to 3% if you put your property in the hands of more than one agent.

Buying through an estate agent

You will receive the following services free:

- Regular pages of property details through the post
- Appointments to view property
- Sale price negotiations with the seller
- Putting your solicitor in touch with the seller's solicitor.

If you do make an offer on a property through an estate agent, he may well ask you for a deposit of £100, which is intended as a demonstration of your intentions. However, make sure that the agent holds your cheque as a stakeholder and doesn't pass it on to the seller. You must also ask for and receive a receipt so that if the sale falls through you get your money back. Recently, some estate agents have asked for a deposit from potential buyers *before* putting in an offer, at the point when they first ask to be put on the agent's list. There's no need to make a deposit of more than £50; if they ask for more, simply negotiate down to £50 and, again, make sure that you get a receipt.

Selling through an estate agent

Usually estate agents' fees vary between 1½ and 3% of the selling price (but when the market is very competitive some will charge only 1%) plus VAT, which some might argue is rather a lot of money for services rendered.

You can decide whether to put your property on one agent's books, or several. Your decision will probably depend on the state of the property market – whether it's a buyer's or seller's. If it's a buyer's market and sales are sluggish, you may think it worth your while to appoint two or three agents in the hope of spreading your net. If this is the case, you'll have to pay a commission of 2½–3% to the successful agent which will cost you:

Sale price	1½%	2%
£35,000	£525	£700
£40,000	£600	£800
£50,000	£750	£1,000
£60,000	£900	£1,200
£70,000	£1,050	£1,400

If, on the other hand, there are people queuing to view property and it's a seller's market, the chances are that you'll only need the services of one agent to move your property quickly and pay a commission of 1½–2%:

Sale price	2½%	3%
£35,000	£875	£1,050
£40,000	£1,000	£1,200
£50,000	£1,250	£1,500
£60,000	£1,500	£1,800
£70,000	£1,750	£2,100

The money is paid to the estate agent on the completion of the sale, less any deposit which you have already paid him. Included in the estate agent's commission are the following services:

- Measuring and valuing your property
- Arranging for your property to be photographed
- Producing typed details for purchasers
- Inserting advertisements in local newspapers
- Arranging viewing times and taking prospective buyers round the property
- Negotiating the sale price
- Contacting solicitors

What's included in the sale price?

When you agree the sale price of a property, whether you're buying or selling, it's quite often the practice to include certain fixtures and fittings in that price. This may serve as an enticement – you may be willing to pay a bit more for the property if you can move in to one which is already carpeted, for instance. Or, it may be a cash basis agreement between buyer and seller after the sale price has already been determined.

If you're selling you may be moving to a new property which already contains some fixtures and fittings which suit your needs, or perhaps the different size of floor area, windows and so on will render your current carpets and curtains useless. You will want, therefore, to try and sell your current fixtures and fittings both to provide extra cash and to avoid the expense and nuisance of having them removed.

If you are offered carpets, curtains, bookshelves, etc, within the existing sale price you should consider whether you actually want them. What state is the carpet in, for instance. Is it worn or dirty? Do you like the colour or pattern? The same would apply to curtains. It may suit you to live with these for a few months until you've decided on your own decoration scheme or until you can afford them. But how much is the seller actually asking for them? It may be that he doesn't want to go to the bother and expense of removing them and 'making good' holes in the wall where shelf brackets have been removed, for instance.

So you may wish to consider offering a lower price for the house without fixtures and fittings and negotiate a different purchase price for selected items. If you're setting up a home for the first time items such as carpets, a cooker, a fridge and so on can be very expensive on top of all your other financial commitments, so purchasing these items second-hand within the purchase price – and therefore paid for over a long term by your mortgage – can prove to be very helpful.

When you have decided which furnishings, fixtures and fittings you want to buy or sell and when you have agreed the price with the seller or buyer, you should make a list of the items for your solicitor so that they can be included in the contract. However, if any of the items are sold on a cash basis it need only concern you and the buyer/seller.

The following checklist will help you to make sure exactly what you want and what you've agreed.

Item offered	Do you need it?	Agreed in sale price	Extra cost £
Hall carpet			
Sitting room carpet			
Dining room carpet			
Kitchen lino/tiles			
Lavatory lino/carpet			
Stair carpet			
Bedroom 1 carpet			
Bedroom 2 carpet			
Bedroom 3 carpet			
Bathroom carpet			
Other room(s) carpet			
Sitting room curtains			
Dining room curtains			
Kitchen curtains/blinds			
Landing curtains			
Bedroom 1 curtains			
Bedroom 2 curtains			
Bedroom 3 curtains			
Lavatory curtains/blinds			
Bathroom curtains/blinds			
Other room(s) curtains			
Cooker			
Fridge			
Freezer			
Washing machine			
Dishwasher			
Tumbledrier			
Bookshelves			
Bathroom shelves			
Lightshades			
Bathroom cabinet			
Kitchen cabinets			

Bridging loans

Bridging loans, as you might expect, are used to bridge the gap between two financial transactions. For instance, you will have to pay the balance of the full purchase price of your new home on the day of completion, but you may not have received the mortgage money from your lender because for one reason or another part or all the advance is being withheld.

Of course, the necessity for a bridging loan does not arise in every property purchasing transaction. One of the most common uses for a bridging loan is when the lender retains some of the mortgage until certain, stipulated repairs have been carried out on the property.

A second use for a bridging loan is paying for a new property before you've sold your old home. This can occur because of a hold up in a chain with the result that there's a gap between the two completion dates.

There is a third occasion when you might need a bridging loan, this is if you haven't saved the 5 or 10% deposit required on exchange of contracts, or if it's tied up in your current property. However, in March 1985 the Deposit Guarantee Scheme was introduced, which means that your solicitor arranges a guarantee for the amount of the deposit, on your behalf. This guarantee is sent to the seller's solicitor at exchange of contract. The cost of this is usually cheaper than a bank's charges – £28 for a deposit guarantee worth £2,000 for a first-time buyer and £20 for a second-time buyer. Nevertheless, it's worth checking with the bank to compare costs, and not all solicitors operate the Deposit Guarantee Scheme.

A bank will provide the finance for a bridging loan, usually at a rate of interest which is lower than that on an overdraft but still 3–4% above current base rate. You don't have to accept the rate offered by the bank – it sometimes pays off to negotiate a lower rate with the manager. In addition, the bank will charge you an arrangement fee somewhere in the region of £75 to £150.

How a bridging loan works

When you reach the stage in your purchase where you can foresee that a bridging loan is unavoidable, you should contact your bank manager to discuss the feasibility of a bridging loan, then, regardless of whether you will eventually need one, you will have the security of knowing that the facility is there. If you are in any doubt about the necessity for a bridging loan, or you're not sure about approaching a bank, your solicitor will be able to give you advice.

Once you have agreed a loan with your bank manager, and the rate of interest which you will pay, ask him to open a separate account for the loan. This is because you can claim tax relief on the interest. (This has to be claimed through your tax office as it does not come under the MIRAS scheme.) In addition to the interest, you will also have to pay an arrangement fee, whether or not you actually use the bridging loan.

When your mortgage retention or proceeds from the sale of your house come through, you simply pay off the loan and close the loan account. If you are paying off the loan on completion, the bridging loan will continue for five days after the date of completion, still incurring interest, as it takes that time to be processed.

Employer loan

For some people, an alternative worth considering is to approach an employer for a bridging loan rather than a bank. He may agree to advance you the money at a lower rate of interest, or even interest-free. If you are being relocated by your firm, it's more than likely that the onus to provide a bridging loan is on them.

Building society or bank?

The most important question you have to ask yourself is how much can you afford to pay? To arrive at that figure, however, you will have to take into account not just the cost of a mortgage but also all the associated costs of buying a property and then the running costs once you have found one. If that sounds daunting, don't worry. Careful planning and sensible estimates will produce a price you can afford for the home of your dreams.

Having decided that you can afford to enter the property market or, if you're already a home-owner, sell your existing property and buy another, you are then faced with more decisions. Who should you approach for a mortgage? What type of mortgage would best suit you? What is a mortgage?

To answer the last question first, a mortgage is a loan with which to buy a property and you undertake to repay the loan, with interest, in monthly instalments.

You may have been saving with a building society or bank for some time in order to help with the purchase of your home and so your first instinct is to approach the institution with which you've saved. The chances are that you will get your mortgage from them. However, if you are prepared to take the time to do some research you may find that you can get better rates elsewhere, another building society for instance, or an insurance company, a foreign bank or by using the services of a mortgage broker. Currently, the mortgage market is bouyant and it's in the borrower's interest to shop around as lenders are competing for your business. Although it's always advisable to have saved with a potential lender, it is possible to get 100% advances from some lenders with whom you have had no previous dealings.

There are several different kinds of mortgages to choose from, too: repayment, endowment, pension-linked and unit-linked, each with varying features to suit different fianancial requirements.

Then you have to come to grips with other ingredients in the mortgage mix, such as the interest rate, the APR, tax relief under MIRAS, arrangement fees; the expense incurred by using the services of an estate agent (if you're selling), solicitors' and surveyor's fees. Then there is stamp duty to pay, a land registry fee, a search fee and removal costs. The list may seem endless but in the following pages you'll find the information and checklists which will help you to plan your finances to the last penny.

Interest rate

Building societies and banks set their interest rates in relation to the base rate and other lenders tend to follow, varying within a band of about 1½%. You've probably either read or heard on the news about the changes which take place in interest rates. You know the sort of thing: the bank base rate rises to 11% and, within a few days, one of the large building societies announces that mortgage interest rates will have to rise from 11% to 12¼%. The other societies then tend to follow suit.

The reason for this is the competition for savings. When the bank base rate rises, savers can be offered higher interest on their savings and, conversely, borrowers have to pay more. Therefore, the building societies are forced to put up their mortgage interest in order to raise their interest to savers and remain competitive with the banks. This doesn't necessarily always happen with a change in base rate: lenders recognise that it might result in hardship and even repossession for some borrowers, and it also costs them quite a lot in terms of administration. When you have a mortgage, and the rate increases (or decreases), the lender will write to you informing you of your new monthly repayment.

Annual percentage rate (APR)

If you possess any credit cards you'll probably be used to this term and it is a better yardstick by which to measure the cost of borrowing. The APR is defined as the annual percentage rate of the total charge for credit. This means that building societies, who calculate interest payments annually, will charge interest on the outstanding mortgage debt at the beginning of the year, not taking into account the fact that during that year you will be repaying some of the loan. Most of the banks base their charge on a monthly rate so that their APR is lower than that of the building societies.

Mortgage term

This is the period over which you repay your loan, most commonly 25 years, although it can be fewer or more years if necessary. It's quite common for someone to sell their house or flat after three years and move to a larger one with a new mortgage. In this case some lenders will charge an early redemption penalty.

Other mortgage sources

In addition to the 200 or so building societies, UK and foreign banks to whom you can apply for a mortgage, there are also over 100 insurance companies, numerous finance companies, builders, local authorities and sometimes employers who are in the mortgage business too. Just to make things more confusing, they offer different types of packages which include varying interest rates, repayment terms, advances, flexibility and so on.

Mortgage and insurance brokers
One way to avoid detailed research and evaluation of these different sources of mortgages is to go to a mortgage or insurance broker. As the term 'broker' suggests, he is a middleman and does not lend money himself but arranges for you to borrow from someone else. As well as steering you towards a source of finance he should also be able to give you advice as to which sort of mortgage – repayment or endowment for instance – best suits your pocket and circumstances. He may also be able to arrange a top-up loan with a company which is approved by the building society with which you have already arranged a mortgage.

Needless to say, not all brokers are good ones and so it's best to ask your solicitor or accountant if he can recommend one, or a friend who has used a broker and found him satisfactory. Alternatively, there are professional insurance bodies to whom you can apply for a list of members: The Corporation of Insurance and Financial Advisors and the British Insurance Brokers' Association (see **Useful addresses** [pp. 188–189]). However, mortgage brokers have no such governing body – anyone can call themselves a mortgage broker, so tread carefully. Some of the larger mortgage broking companies run very good broking services and will give you a very firm guiding hand through the minefield of what you can afford, your borrowing requirement, the most suitable mortgage and methods of repayment. They charge you nothing on an endowment mortgage (they get their commission from the insurance companies) and 1% of a repayment mortgage.

Insurance companies
Recently, insurance companies have entered the mortgage market in strength. Previously very few gave first mortgages and concentrated more on top-up loans for existing life insurance policyholders, but now some 100 companies are prepared to offer first-time buyers mortgages, either directly or through insurance and mortgage brokers.

Normally, insurance companies only offer endowment mortgages linked to a life insurance policy or pension-linked mortgages.

It's important to chose a good insurance company with a sound track record as some tend to advertise incredible growths and targets without ever achieving them. (The insurance industry has recently agreed on new, more prudent projections in their advertising but it will still pay to look at past performance.)

Local authorities

Under current legislation, local authorities are legally required to provide a mortgage for a council tenant who wants to buy his or her council home. They will also lend to other sorts of buyers but not on a large scale and the willingness to do so varies from authority to authority.

On the whole, they prefer lending to someone who cannot find mortgage funding elsewhere (for valid reasons) so, if all else fails, it's worth asking. You can find out details and costs by applying to the treasurer's department at your local town hall.

Usually, local authorities are willing to lend money on properties with sitting tenants, or where the buyer intends improving a property within the authority's area. Again, each authority decides on its own lending rules. The amount you can borrow will be determined up to the same limits as a building society but the interest will probably be higher.

Builders

If you are buying a property on a brand new development you may well find that you can arrange a mortgage with the builders or developers (and in times of great competition, often with fixtures, fittings and a bottle of champagne thrown in!).

Other mortgage sources (cont.)

Employers
If you're an employee of a bank, building society or insurance company you'll probably be able to get a mortgage with them at a much reduced rate of interest. Lucky you! However, even if you're not, it's still worth speaking to your employer about a mortgage – quite a number of larger firms have schemes. If your employer does offer you finance, find out what your position would be if, for any reason, you left the firm.

Other mortgage lenders
There are two other types of financial institution in the mortgage lending business: finance houses and, a recent development, equity-based mortgage institutions specifically set up to do mortgage business.

Finance houses are, strictly speaking, credit companies which finance hire purchase operations, store credit cards for instance, or car HP or leasing. They tend to consider property purchasing along the same lines so their interest rates tend to be higher than other sources, although to be fair, they're becoming increasingly competitive. They are more useful as sources for second mortgages or top-up loans.

Mortgage institutions are comparatively new sorts of lender which raise funds by issuing marketable securities and lend them directly to homeowners. One such institution is the Household Mortgage Corporation (HMC), which has no branch network and mainly uses estate agents, insurance companies and mortgage brokers as intermediaries although you can apply direct. At the time of writing, they offer the lowest variable interest rate on the market.

Practically all these lending sources, like the building societies and the banks, have speeded up their services to attract more customers.

Evaluating your mortgage offer(s)
The following checklists may help you through the maze of deciding where to look for a likely mortgage offer and how to evaluate the different offers.

Type of lender	Repayment Mortgage Int. rate	Endowment Mortgage Int. rate	Maximum Advance	Maximum Term	Further Inf.
Building society					
UK clearing bank					
UK branch foreign bank					
Insurance company					
Employer					
Local authority					
Builder/ developer					
Finance company					
Mortgage corporation					

Advisor	Type of broker recommended	Approached		Advice offered	
Solicitor		Yes	No	Yes	No
Accountant		Yes	No	Yes	No
Bank manager		Yes	No	Yes	No
Friend		Yes	No	Yes	No
Estate agent		Yes	No	Yes	No

Buying a retirement home

If you are retiring or, for that matter, retired, you may be thinking of buying a retirement home or moving into a smaller residence. This is a growing and competitive area of the housing market and there is plenty on offer to suit all tastes and needs, including financial packages tailored for retirement income.

Even if you are selling your own home to purchase a smaller bungalow-type home and hoping to realise quite a large proportion of capital as you have paid off your mortgage, it may still be worth your while looking at retirement home complexes from a practicable point of view, eg wardens on site, shopping facilities and so on.

Sheltered housing schemes

There are over 900 sheltered housing schemes in the UK, offering over 30,000 purpose-built units. More and more developments are being planned which are geared not just to the elderly but towards those who view retirement as a time for leisure and enjoyable activities as well. Prices range from about £40,000 for a two-bedroom bungalow to approximately £80,000 for a two-bedroom cottage, depending on the part of the country in which they are situated.

The schemes vary, of course, but many offer services such as hairdressing, chiropody, physiotherapy, on-call nursing care, and even meals. Many developments have additional shared facilities such as lounges and dining rooms where neighbours can get together and never feel lonely.

Usually, these sheltered housing developments are run by housing associations. They would be responsible for standing charges, maintenance and repairs and anything of common interest to all residents such as parking, pets, disputes and so on.

What does the price include?

Most 'sheltered' homes are sold on a lease basis. In addition to the cost of the lease, you will have to pay a service charge which might be between about £7–15 a week and could be subject to annual rises. In some cases, it's possible to get help with this charge from the local DHSS.

Many developments also have what is called a 'sinking fund', which pays for any major repair or improvement work – this might take the form of an additional charge or deferred until such time as your property is sold.

If you wish to resell the property you may find that the lease stipulates that your home can only be sold on to another retired person. Lessees who want to nominate a successor would normally have to get the agreement of the landlord first but, providing that the nominee was a retired person there shouldn't normally be any problem. Before signing any lease you should make sure that you can retain any equity in the increased sale price above the initial purchase price (excluding any sinking fund repairs).

Before purchasing a lease of this sort check exactly what is included in the purchase price and what is extra:

- Service charge
- Repairs and maintenance
- Warden's services
- Equity retention
- Building insurance costs. Is the landlord responsible?

Other provisions of the lease which are worth checking might include:

- Whether the landlord can terminate the lease if you fall ill or become incapacitated
- If there's a 24-hour monitored alarm system
- What the warden's duties are, eg will he or she do shopping, cooking or cleaning?

Paying for your retirement home

Most banks and building societies operate special packages for those who are approaching or are in retirement. Obviously 25 year mortgages are not feasible however famous your family may be for longevity, but there are alternatives. For instance a shorter term top-up/mortgage loan which is based on your pension and other retirement income which is end-loaded, that is to say it will be paid off from your estate when you die.

There is no rule of thumb and your best bet would be to discuss your needs with your bank or building society branch manager. You can obtain further information about sheltered housing in a booklet issued by the House-Builders Federation, called *Sheltered Housing for Sale – An Advice Note*, price £4 (see **Useful addresses** [pp. 188–189])

Second mortgages and top-up loans

Sometimes, for one reason or another, people looking for finance to purchase their home need to find, say, a couple of thousand pounds in addition to a mortgage if the lender is unwilling to advance as much as is needed. When this occurs there are many lenders, normally insurance companies, who will provide top-up loans.

Second mortgages, or further advances as they are sometimes called, are similar to top-up loans and provide a useful source of extra money. They are most often needed when you already own a property. You may need to raise some capital for any number of reasons – to build onto your home or put into a business, for example. Having had a mortgage on your property for, say, five years, the difference between the mortgage and the market value of your home may have increased by quite a significant amount; this is your capital but it's tied up in the property. You can, however, take out a second mortgage based on a valuation and free some of your capital. It is called a second mortgage if you take it out with a different lender from the one who advanced your original mortgage, and a further advance if it's with your current lender.

Just to add to the confusion, there's a third type of loan which is called a re-mortgage. This is when you replace an existing loan with a larger one, but beware of loss of tax relief which is only ever granted when money is spent on the purchase or improvement of property.

Top-up loans

Finance houses, which are nearly all subsidiaries of the main banks, will offer top-up loans. In addition to making up a 100% mortgage where all the finance is not available from your main lender, top-up loans from a finance house can be quite useful in that the rate of interest charged is competitive with the first lender in the region of 95–100% of the advance. Insurance companies will also arrange top-up loans.

Insurance companies, and for that matter any lender of a top-up loan, will probably require you to take out a life insurance policy to cover the cost of the loan should you die before it was repaid. They may also limit the amount of the top-up loan to a certain percentage of your mortgage loan.

Of course, you will have to get approval from the lender of your mortgage to take out a top-up loan because it affects the security of their loan. Some lenders may decide that as they have already made you the maximum mortgage offer which they think you can afford to repay, you would be ill-advised to take out a top-up loan. Or the reason that your mortgage offer is smaller than your requirements is due to the nature of the property and the lender's rules only allows a certain maximum on that type of property. In this case they may be quite happy for you to spread the lending load.

Building societies and banks have their own lists of approved insurance companies and finance houses but you can equally well find out the best deal by consulting a mortgage or insurance broker.

There are usually extra costs involved in arranging a top-up loan. These costs may include an arrangement fee, the lender's solicitor's costs and your solicitor's costs.

Second mortgage or further advance

If, for example, you bought a house for £35,000 five years ago with a mortgage of £30,000, the house might now be revalued at say £50,000. This means that you have an equity of £20,000, most of which could be used as security for a second loan, in other words a second mortgage or further advance.

Finance houses are a good source of lending for second mortgages. They only charge an arrangement fee, in other words there are no legal fees or incidental costs involved. As you might expect, the interest rate charged is usually higher than that charged on a first mortgage, to cover the additional risk. The repayment term is generally shorter, too.

Generally, lenders of second mortgages will require you to take additional life insurance to cover the risk.

Home improvement loans

Home improvement can add to the potential sale price of a property or perhaps it is more of an essential repair that you need to carry out, such as a new roof, or just for your own comfort such as a new kitchen. Before embarking on home improvement and seeking the necessary finance it is worth considering whether you hope to add to your sale price by carrying out the improvement and, if so, will it?

A new garage or a new room extension will probably be a good investment, though it may take a few years to realise the profit. If you live in an area where most of the houses have garages and you don't you may well have to drop your sale price significantly. Similarly, central heating is a more common pre-requisite of a property these days and if you install this with a view to selling within two to three years you'll probably get a better sale price than if you didn't.

The most common home improvements in the UK are new kitchen/dining room, double glazing, central heating, a new garage and new furniture and carpets.

A further advance

A way of paying for home improvements is to obtain a further advance from your mortgage lender or another financial institution. This will spread the cost over the length of your mortgage term, making it a more expensive loan in the long term but bearable in the short, especially if the loan qualifies for the MIRAS scheme and tax relief. Some improvements, eg furniture and carpets do not, but others such as extensions do qualify; your lender will be able to clarify this for you.

Sometimes it is possible to get local grants towards the cost of home improvements if the work you want to carry out helps to improve the fundamental nature of the property and thus reflects well on the area, for instance a new roof or installing an inside lavatory or an upstairs bathroom. Your local town hall will have details of any grants which they may offer.

Before carrying out the work, consult your lender. He may require several estimates from contractors or he may want to send round a representative to ensure that the work is necessary. (Too many people have sought home improvement loans to obtain a tax-free new car!)

How much can I borrow?

As long as the amount of your further advance added to what is outstanding on your mortgage doesn't exceed the total value of your home, you can apply for any amount you can afford. Obviously, the same restrictions apply as those for a mortgage application, eg your annual income, etc. If the two sums come close to the sale value of your home, the lender may commission a valuation for which you will be charged. Use the following checklist to calculate your home improvement potential:

Home improvement required
☐ New kitchen/ dining area
☐ Double-glazing
☐ Central heating
☐ Garage
☐ Bedroom extension
☐ New furniture/ carpets
☐ New windows/ patio doors
☐ New bathroom
☐ Inside lavatory
☐ Redecoration
☐ Outside extension
☐ Utility room
☐ Loft conversion
☐ Swimming pool

How much will the improvement cost		
Estimates obtained: (1) £...................... (3) £...................... (2) £......................		
Is there a local government grant available?	**Yes**	**No**
Home improvement loan applied for?	**Yes**	**No**
Related costs	**£**	
Estimated cost of home improvement less any government grant		
Valuation fee		
Buildings insurance		
Loan arrangement fee		
Solicitor's fee		
Loan required		
Will the loan qualify for tax relief?	**Yes**	**No**
Monthly repayments	**£**	
Monthly loan repayment		
Monthly mortgage repayment		
Total monthly repayments		
Estimated increase in sale value:	**Yes**	**No**

Mortgage repayment difficulties

In this section you may have noticed that we have emphasised one point on several occasions and that is do not be tempted to pay more than you can afford. In times of competition between lenders it seems that they will go to any lengths to woo the borrower, and this sometimes unfortunately includes lending more than borrowers can afford, with disastrous consequences.

For example, a couple each earning £10,000 might be offered a mortgage of £25,000 from one lender – 2½ times one salary – or £50,000 by another. It is obvious that the second figure is far more likely to stretch their financial resources than the first, and it can only be described as irresponsible lending.

However, blame cannot be completely landed at the door of the lenders. It's easy to get carried away when you've found a house or flat that you really want. You may kid yourself that your salary will go up, that you can cut down on certain luxuries and so on. Do bear in mind, however, that over the past two years there has been a dramatic increase in repossession of property by lenders – over 16,000 homes were repossessed in 1985 – because borrowers defaulted on mortgage payments. This has partly been due to increases in unemployment but the underlying trend is that people have been taking on larger mortgages than they can afford.

What happens if you cannot pay your mortgage?

If you find that the running costs of your new home are higher than you expected, or if perhaps the mortgage rate goes up and you cannot meet the monthly payments, contact your lender at once. Most lenders, especially the building societies and banks, will do their utmost to help you replan your finances and your monthly payments. They have no desire to push you out of your home, not only for humane reasons, but also it would be an expensive operation to get a court order for repossession, and put the property on the market again to discharge the mortgage.

They may, for instance, be able to extend the term of the mortgage from 25 to 30 years, which would bring down the monthly payments to within manageable proportions, although it would make the cost of buying the property more expensive in the long term.

If you are made redundant, you can sort out the problem with your lender and the Department of Health and Social Security (DHSS). Usually, the DHSS will pay your mortgage for you for up to six months while you look for another job (you will, of course, have to repay this benefit). If, at the end of six months, you are in the unfortunate position of having found no new employment, the lender may have to give you warning of repossession. You may have decided to sell the property anyway, in the hope that prices have risen sufficiently for you to completely discharge your mortgage and pay for the expenses of selling.

Should you foresee any problem arising with your ability to meet mortgage payments in the long term, and if you do not have friends or relatives with whom you can move in, it is a wise precaution to put yourself on the council waiting list for council accommodation. If your situation improves, you can always take your name off the list but if it doesn't you won't face eviction without anywhere else to live.

Repossession

In the sad event that you cannot afford to keep your home, the mortgagee will seek a court order for repossession. You will be given notice to quit the premises, and the lender, who holds the title deeds to your property, will have the legal right to discharge your mortgage by putting your home on the market again.

Will it happen to you?

Although there has been such a marked increase in repossessions, the likelihood of this happening to you is slim if you bear the following points in mind:

- Don't obtain a bigger mortgage than you can comfortably afford. The onus is on you to decide how much that is but a responsible lender will help you to plan your finances realistically.
- If spending less means that you have set your sights lower in the property market, then do so. It's better to have two bedrooms than none at all.
- If you do have problems with your monthly payments do not be afraid to let your lender know and discuss the situation with them fully. They will help as much as they can to ease the burden and avoid repossession.

SECTION FIVE

THE LEGAL SIDE

Property law in England and Wales has developed over centuries and the process of transferring property from one person to another is quite complicated, if only from an administrative point of view. The legal work involved in this transfer is called conveyancing and you will have to choose whether to do this yourself or appoint a solicitor or legal conveyancer to carry out the work on your behalf.

Much property in England and Wales has what is called registered title. This means that details of past transactions such as sales, mortgages on the property and rights and restrictions are recorded in the Land Registry and may be inspected by anyone authorised by the owner. The main reason for this is to prevent someone purporting to sell a property he does not own.

When you buy a property, you want to be sure that you are getting value for money, and that what you see and make an offer for is what you get. This means that there are various precautions you or your solicitor have to take before entering into an exchange of contracts, which is legally binding.

You will have visited the property and made what can only be described as a rudimentary inspection. Your offer will be based partly on a practical level and partly emotional. Therefore, your surveyor will do a structural survey to ensure that the fabric is sound and your solicitor will, so to speak, carry out a legal survey to make sure that the purchase is watertight legally.

The steps that you and your solicitor will take are as follows:

1 You appoint a solicitor to do your conveyancing work.

2 You put an offer in on a property and, when this has been accepted, you give details of the estate agent and the seller to your solicitor.

3 The estate agent will inform the seller's solicitor who will then send a draft contract to your solicitor.

4 In response to the draft contract your solicitor will send the seller's solicitor a set of preliminary enquiries. These will aim to elicit answers to various technicalities raised by the contract. This can sometimes take quite a bit of paper shuffling between the two sets of solicitors.

5 Meanwhile your solicitor will make searches in the Land Charges Registry (where title is not registered) or in the Land Registry (where it is) to find out if there are any prior charges on the property or any other matters adversely affecting it, and with the Local Authority to discover if, for instance, there is any redevelopment planned in your street, or the road is due to be widened.

6 If necessary, your solicitor will also have given you advice on where to seek a mortgage and/or bridging loan.
7 Most of the major building societies and the clearing banks will usually instruct your solicitor (but no other legal adviser) to represent them also in the transaction of completing your mortgage. In the few cases where this is not so, your solicitor will arrange for the lender's solicitors to have access to the enquiries he has made so that they can satisfy themselves that the property will be a suitable security for their client's loan to you.
8 You will have to arrange that you have funds available to pay the deposit on exchange of contracts.
9 When your solicitor is satisfied that your mortgage is forthcoming, that all his preliminary enquiries have been properly answered, and his searches have proved satisfactory, you will exchange contracts with the seller.
10 You are now legally bound to complete the purchase and failure to do so can be very expensive.
11 Following exchange of contract, your solicitor will again make searches where necessary with the Land Charges or Land Registries and he will also investigate the title to make sure that the seller is the owner.
12 If separately represented, the mortgage lender's solicitor will send your solicitor further enquiries which he will have to answer.
13 If you already have a mortgage on the property you are selling, he will arrange to discharge it on completion, simultaneously with the completion of your purchase and new mortgage.
14 You will have to send your solicitor the balance of the purchase price.
15 Your lender will send the mortgage money to your solicitor who will send the money to the seller's solicitors.
16 The seller's solicitor will send your solicitor the title deeds and conveyance or transfer and the keys will be handed to you, usually by the seller direct or his estate agent.
17 Your solicitor will send in his bill if he has not already done so.
18 Your solicitor will send the conveyance or transfer to the Inland Revenue with a cheque to cover stamp duty. They will impress it and return it to your solicitor or your mortgagee's solicitor.
19 The transfer of title will be recorded in the Land Registry where the title is registered.

Choosing a solicitor

A solicitor is a professional and has to abide by a strict code of practice so you shouldn't have any problems finding a good one. However, in order to be a 100% sure that you have the right man or woman for the job, it's safer not to just walk into the first solicitor's office that you see but to go through one of the following channels:

- a recommendation from a friend, relative or colleague who has used the solicitor in the past;
- a recommendation from your bank manager, your building society manager or possibly your estate agent;
- a recommendation from your local Citizen's Advice Bureau.

Alternatively, you can ask a conveyancer to deal with your purchase. Conveyancers have legal knowledge but they aren't qualified solicitors. You should choose one who has at least five years' experience, has professional indemnity and fidelity insurance and who keeps a separate client's account. Currently, conveyancers have to rely on solicitors for some part of the legal work but in 1987 a bill will be enacted allowing them to perform the whole procedure. To choose a reliable conveyancer, contact the National Association of Conveyancers (see **Useful addresses** [pp. 188–189]). It is doubtful, however, whether banks or building societies will instruct conveyancers to act on their behalf even after the act comes into force. Thus separate solicitors for your mortgagee are still likely to be instructed for whom you will be expected to pay.

You can opt to use the building society's or bank's solicitors if you choose to acquire your mortgage through them. What you cannot do is use the same solicitor as the seller as this would cause a conflict of interests. If you're both selling and buying, the same solicitor can handle both transactions for you.

Where your solicitor is located is not of paramount importance although it sometimes helps if he works in the same area where you're buying as he may have useful contacts in the local land registry, or the building societies for instance. It is probably much more important for you to use a solicitor who is conveniently located for you to see and speak to during the transaction.

One of the key factors which you will probably take into account when choosing your solicitor, is his fee. Fees can vary but the standard fee is usually between ½% and 1% plus VAT of the purchase price. Some solicitors will quote a rate in advance, others a flat fee and still others may determine their fee according to how complicated the transaction proves to be. If you feel that you have been overcharged you have recourse to the Law Society who will review your case. In such a case, you should, within 28 days of your solicitor delivering his bill to you, ask him in writing to obtain from the Law Society, a "Certificate of Reasonableness" of his fees.

Use the following chart to sort out your criteria in choosing a solicitor; it would be worth your while finding three to ring up and then make a comparison.

Solicitor A: .... Tel no: .... Recommended by	Fee £............ Plus approximate sum for disbursements £............	
Can he arrange a mortgage? If yes, with whom?	**Yes**	**No**
Does he operate the Deposit Guarantee Scheme?	**Yes**	**No**
Does he know the area in which the property is situated?	**Yes**	**No**

Solicitor B: .... Tel no: .... Recommended by	Fee £............ Plus approximate sum for disbursements £............	
Can he arrange a mortgage? If yes, with whom?	**Yes**	**No**
Does he operate the Deposit Guarantee Scheme?	**Yes**	**No**
Does he know the area in which the property is situated?	**Yes**	**No**

Solicitor C: .... Tel no: .... Recommended by	Fee £............ Plus approximate sum for disbursements £............	
Can he arrange a mortgage? If yes, with whom?	**Yes**	**No**
Does he operate the Deposit Guarantee Scheme?	**Yes**	**No**
Does he know the area in which the property is situated?	**Yes**	**No**

Your first consultation

If you haven't been through the process of buying a home before, you should ask your solicitor to give you an explanation of the process and the part he will play in the purchase. This can be a very active one as he may be able to arrange a mortgage for you if you haven't already found one elsewhere – he or she probably knows the local bank and building society managers or a mortgage broker on a sound professional basis. The solicitor can guide you through the pitfalls which can occur, such as gazumping or a bad survey, and will generally relieve you of some of the worry which buying a home can cause.

Questions you should ask

Find out about any potential legal snags which your purchase might entail. Although your solicitor will carry out a local search, he may have some prior knowledge of the district or road in which you hope to buy. For instance, a redevelopment or plans to widen the road, the introduction of a one-way system, local planning restrictions if you'd thought of extending the property, and so on. If he has the answer to any of these queries at this stage it will save you the expense and heartbreak of carrying on any further with a particular property.

Ask your solicitor for a rough schedule of the process. If you're selling and buying this can be quite tricky because of the 'chain' effect; in other words you are reliant on other sellers and buyers and you need to know how to handle the balancing act of exchange of contracts. You should also ask whether the solicitor is willing to arrange a deposit guarantee as this will save you going to the expense of a bridging loan. Your solicitor may point out to you that, for one reason or another, you will need a bridging loan, so make sure you ask him at this stage so that you can arrange it, thereby saving valuable time rather than arranging one at the last minute and holding up the proceedings.

If you haven't arranged a mortgage, ask the solicitor for his advice. He might be able to advise you about what you can afford and to whom you should apply, especially if he's on a building society panel. He can also recommend a surveyor if you want a full survey done of the property.

Finally, you could ask your solicitor if he can give you a rough idea of the extra costs entailed in the conveyancing, such as solicitor's disbursements (for instance he may charge you for telephone calls, letters, couriers, etc), search fees, stamp duty and land registry fees.

First consultation

Here is a checklist to help you through your first consultation with your solicitor:

Solicitor's name: ....

Telephone number: ....

Appointment arranged for: .... time: ....

Are there any legal snags that he can foresee? eg building restrictions, redevelopments	**Yes**	**No**
Will I need a bridging loan?	**Yes**	**No**
If yes, can he help to arrange it?	**Yes**	**No**
Can he arrange a mortgage:	**Yes**	**No**
Can he recommend a surveyor: If yes, name:	**Yes**	**No**

How long does he think it will take to do the searches? ....
When will exchange of contracts take place? ....
When will completion take place? ....
When will I need to pay the solicitor's fees? ....

How much will I have to pay for	(a) search fees?	
	(b) disbursements?	
	(c) land registry fees?	
	(d) stamp duty?	
	(e) solicitor's fee?	
	Total legal cost	

Enquiries before contract

When a seller or his estate agent show you round a property they, naturally enough, are pointing out all the selling features and not the defects. If there are any defects, you may not notice them because they may not be easily visible, ie they may be to do with party walls, or restrictive covenants, or any number of problems. The rule of *caveat emptor* – buyer beware – applies to the sale of land; in other words, you buy at your own risk because although the seller is not entitled to deceive or mislead you, he is not legally bound to voluntarily draw your attention to any defects. This is where enquiries before contract come into play as they aim to discover any defects in the property which you cannot expect to find out by inspecting the property yourself.

The form consists of a series of questions:

1 Boundaries. This is to find out if fences, walls, etc, are the responsibility of the property owner.

2 Disputes. The seller has to note whether there have been any past or current disputes (eg with neighbours) about boundaries, easements (entering into a neighbour's property to unblock a common drain, for instance) and covenants.

3 Notices. Any notices which might affect the use or enjoyment of the property.

4 Guarantees. Are there any existing guarantees on the property, eg for a damp proof course, dry rot extermination, National House Building Council agreements, certificates, etc, insurance policy, guarantee, warranty or insurance policy relating to a defective title, and so on. If so, has any work been carried out under the guarantees, etc.

5 Services. This is to confirm that gas, electricity, drainage and water are all laid on and where and how they enter the property.

6 Exclusive facilities. For instance, is access to the property exclusive?

7 Shared facilities. Are any roads, paths, drains, wire, pipes, party walls and so on shared with other properties?

8 Adverse Rights. Here, the seller is asked if he is aware of any rights or informal arrangements which specifically affect the property.

9 Restrictions. If there are any restrictions, have they been observed?

10 Planning, etc. This is to find out what the property is used for and whether any buildings have been added to or altered and, more to the point, whether planning permission has been obtained or complied with (even if you weren't responsible for circumventing planning, you could still be asked to pull down the offending building).

11 Fixtures, fittings, etc. This is where all the fixtures and fittings which the seller has agreed to include in the sale price should be listed – though it's probably easier to note the items which aren't in the sale price but might be mistakenly thought to be, eg a wall-mounted cupboard or flower tubs.

12 Outgoings. What is the rateable value of the property? Have any works been carried out which might result in revised rates? What annual or periodic charges are there, other than general or water rates (this might include ground rent for instance)?

13 Completion. This is to discover how long after the exchange of contracts the seller will be able to give vacant possession of the property.

14 New properties. This applies to newly-built houses and flats to make certain that the seller – normally a developer – will pay all the charges for constructing and connecting drainage and other services, such as gas, as well as fencing, drives, paths, and so on.

These are the main questions asked in the enquiries before contract, but your solicitor may have additional questions of his own which he will attach to the form. These might include asking the seller whether to the best of his knowledge the property has been affected by subsidence, dry rot or insect infestation; whether the central heating system works properly; has the property been burgled or vandalised?

A seller is not obliged to disclose any physical defect in the property which he's selling unless asked, regardless as to whether it is either what is termed a 'latent' or hidden, physical defect – loose roof tiles for example – or a 'patent', or obvious, physical defect, eg missing roof tiles. You or your surveyor are supposed to pick up these problems. However, if the seller deliberately misrepresents or misleads you and this becomes apparent after contracts have been exchanged, you may be able to rescind the contract or sue for damages.

Enquiries before contract can take some time, especially if your solicitor isn't fully satisfied by the replies he receives to his questions. He may well return to the seller's solicitor with further supplementary questions. If he still receives unsatisfactory information he may well suggest that you withdraw your offer for that property. You don't have to take his advice, but you may think twice about buying a property which, when you come to sell, may prove difficult with your buyer and his solicitor.

Tying up the loose ends

In addition to the more obvious tasks which your solicitor carries out on your behalf, he will also be busy behind the scenes tying up loose ends. This will especially be the case if you are buying a leasehold flat or a new property.

A new house
There are a number of points which your solicitor will have to check because, as it's a newly-built property, they won't have been covered before. For instance, he'll have to ensure that the contract actually includes a covenant by the developer that the house is properly built and that appropriate services such as electricity, gas and water are laid on. He'll discover and tell you if there are any restrictions affecting the property. For instance, you might not be allowed to erect a greenhouse or keep a large pet. Roads and access will have to be checked to ensure that they will be built if they haven't already, and that arrangements have been made for them to be adopted and maintained by the local council after the developer has withdrawn. He'll also want to check a plan to make sure that your boundaries are clearly marked and cannot be misinterpreted at a later date.

Leasehold flat
As you might expect, where a leasehold property is concerned, your solicitor will have to take a toothcomb through the small print of the lease to ensure that it is satisfactory. He will ascertain the ground rent payable and check that there are adequate covenants to take care of all repairs, maintenance and upkeep of the fabric of the building in which the flat is situated. He should also try to discover whether there are any outstanding breaches of covenant. There may be an additional service charge for a porter, lifts, garden maintenance, and so on.

Surveyor's report
While your solicitor is making his preliminary enquiries, you will have instructed a surveyor to carry out a structural survey of the property. His report may include several recommendations which could affect the price so you should give a copy of the report to your solicitor so that he can advise you what course of action to take. He may recommend that you renegotiate the sale price. Any change in price, or agreement that you reach with the seller, for instance if he agrees to carry out the repairs at his expense before completion, will have to be entered in the contract.

Rates

When you received agent's details of the property, they should have contained the rateable value. This, however, does not tell you how much your rates will cost and if the seller doesn't have this information to hand, your solicitor will be able to work it out for you. He may recommend that the rates are too high and that it would be worth your while to ask the local authority rating officer to inspect the property and reassess your rates. Use this table to check that you are keeping up to date with your solicitor's findings.

New House:		
Are there any restrictions which might affect the decision to pursue the purchase?	**Yes**	**No**
Will all services be laid on by completion date?	**Yes**	**No**
Who will be responsible for maintaining roads?		
Any other comments?	**Yes**	**No**
Decide to continue with purchase?	**Yes**	**No**

Leasehold flat:		
Is the ground rent acceptable?	**Yes**	**No**
What service does it include?		
Are there any additional maintenance costs?	**Yes**	**No**
Are there any restrictions?	**Yes**	**No**
Decide to continue with purchase?	**Yes**	**No**

Survey Report:			
Are there any recommendations?		**Yes**	**No**
If yes: solicitor advises:	(a) negotiate price down	**Yes**	**No**
	(b) seller must complete repairs at his own cost	**Yes**	**No**
	(c) repairs done at your cost	**Yes**	**No**
	(d) withdraw offer.	**Yes**	**No**

Will:		
Ask solicitor to draw up will pending completion of purchase?	**Yes**	**No**

Registry/local authority searches

These searches are carried out on your behalf by your solicitor to ensure that nothing is registered against the property in the register of local land charges and nothing adverse is planned locally which might affect the home you are about to buy. For instance, you might think twice about buying it if you found that the council planned to widen the road and cut your front garden in half. Or, the land on which your house or flat stands is about to be compulsorily purchased, or the property has been condemned as unfit for human habitation! These are not 'fail safe' searches because the situation only applies on the day that the searches are made. The next day a very different picture may apply.

A search results in an official certificate showing entries on what is called the local land charges register on the day of the search. A local land charges register is kept by every local authority to show what, if any, obligations the local authority or other authorities can impose on you when you own the property. These charges are usually in the interest of the public generally – for instance you may not be allowed to cut down trees in your garden. Or, the planning register may place restrictions on the use of your property.

In addition to the local authority, there may be other authorities who have a charge on the land register. For instance, the local water board may have the right to dig up your garden to get at pipes or the Civil Aviation Board may have registered a charge to compulsorily purchase your house to make way for a new airport. Once you own your property there's nothing you can do to prevent those with prior charges on the land register from carrying out their intentions. The best you can hope for is decent compensation.

There are two sorts of charges, restrictive and financial. A restrictive charge is one which prevents you from doing certain things. A very common one in most towns and cities occurs in what's commonly known as the smokeless zone, whereby you are not allowed to burn fuel in your home if it gives off any smoke. If you have a hedge you may have to keep it trimmed back so that it doesn't grow out into the street and get in the way of pedestrians. Or, again, the property which you intend buying may be a 'listed' one – of historical or architectural importance – so you will be prevented from making changes to the structure.

Financial charges, on the other hand, are for the protection of the local authority if you fail to comply with various acts of parliament to do with public health, roads, safety, etc. If, through your negligence, the local authority is forced to carry out some action which entails expenditure on their part, you will have to pay and, if you fail to do so, they have a charge on your property. Your search will discover if such a financial charge exists on the property and, if there is, your solicitor will insist that the seller pays it off before any contract is exchanged.

Speeding up the searches

Depending on your local authority, searches can take from between two weeks and three months. A number of the borough councils in London, in particular, can delay your purchase by anything up to three months as they are either overwhelmed with enquiries or give searches a very low priority. The process can be speeded up by doing a personal search.

Normally, your solicitor will send the forms to the local authority for completion by them. He normally has a good idea of which authorities are speedy in replying and those who are not and, if your purchase relies on a rapid exchange of contracts, he may suggest that he hires the services of a law agency representative to pursue the matter in person, or you can opt to do the searches yourself.

If you decide to do the search yourself you should bear the following points in mind:

- Check which council you should apply to.
- Check with the council that they will allow you to do the search and make an appointment.
- If you do a personal search you run a risk of not having done it throughly enough through sheer lack of experience.
- If a search is done by post the local authority is liable for mistakes made and they would have to compensate you. This is not the case if you do a personal search.
- If you are obtaining a mortgage through a building society, their solicitor will want proper searches carried out and therefore a personal search will not be accepted. In such cases there is really nothing you can do to speed up your transaction if the local authority is being very slow.

Investigation of title

The saying goes that an Englishman's castle is his home. But is it? How can you prove that the person from whom you are buying the property is actually the owner? What's to stop a confidence trickster from selling you a stranger's house and you finding yourself homeless and broke?

Proof of ownership
The title or deeds to a property is proof of ownership. When you have given your solicitor instructions to do the conveyancing on a property which you want to buy, one of the things which he will do on your behalf is to investigate the title.

The Land Registry
Title to property can either be registered or unregistered. About 85% of property in England and Wales is registered as a result of the 1925 Land Registration Act. The idea behind this Act was to replace individual investigation of a title with a title (once registered) guaranteed by the state. Land registration is administered by the Land Registry, which is situated in London with district registries all over England and Wales. Land registration in Scotland only began in 1980, but in England and Wales it has been in existence since 1840. Even so not all of the country is registered and there are still parts where registration is still not compulsory.

All transactions which affect the title of a property which is subject to registration are recorded on the register, such as the transfer of ownership, mortgages, covenants, changes in boundaries and so on. The owners of all registered property are issued with a land certificate by the Land Registry which shows all details of the entries in the register relating to their property. The certificate itself comprises a booklet divided into three sections: Section A contains a description of the property together with the benefit of any rights enjoyed by it (ie, rights of way over adjoining land); Section B records the owners of the property and any changes in them; Section C records any matters to which the property is subject, ie mortgages, covenants or rights over it, etc. There is also a plan attached showing the property, called 'the filed plan'. Every time there is a dealing with the land the certificate must be returned to the Registry for amendment.

Registered property
The investigation of a seller's title takes place after exchange of contracts. If the property you are purchasing has a registered title,

the seller's solicitor will send to your solicitor's office copies of the entries on the register, the filed plan of the property and any relevant documents noted on the register, as well as all authority to inspect the register. Your solicitor will have to make sure that no changes have taken place on the register since the date the copies were issued.

All Land Registry searches are made by postal application. The chances are that the certificate of official search which your solicitor will be sent by the Registry will state that there have been no adverse entries recorded. If the current owner of the property has a mortgage on it, this will be recorded on the register and your solicitor will have to make sure that this is discharged before the title is transferred to you.

Your lender's solicitor will also need to know that there have been no adverse entries against your property in the register, so their solicitor will also apply for an official search on their behalf.

In either case the authority of the seller's solicitor is required to search as the register is not open to public search.

Unregistered property

If the property is unregistered, the process of proving title to ownership is more complicated.

The seller's solicitor will send your solicitor a summary of the title deeds going back at least 15 years. Your solicitor will then have to investigate these, for instance making sure that the property has been properly transferred during that period and checking on the rights of way, drainage, boundaries, and so on. He will do this by searching the Land Charges Registry, which is a government department in Plymouth, where details of certain matters affecting unregistered property are held and recorded under the name of the owner and not the property. Inevitably, this will entail more work and your solicitor will charge accordingly.

To register an unregistered property

Land registration is now compulsory in many parts of England and Wales, so if you buy an unregistered property in an area of compulsory registration, you will have to register your title.

Your solicitor will have to investigate it as unregistered land and when the title has been transferred to you, he will register the title at the Land Registry. The Registry will charge you a fee for this, based on the amount you paid for the property, but it will be less than the fee for transferring a registered property to a new owner.

Paying the deposit

When contracts are exchanged, your solicitor will need to send your deposit to the seller's solicitor. After contracts have been exchanged you are bound by it and must proceed. You will lose that deposit if you withdraw from the sale after exchange has taken place, unless, that is, the seller is in default.

The normal requirement is that the deposit should be 10% of the selling price, so if you are buying a house, say, for £52,000, you would have to pay a deposit of £5,200 less any deposit which you may have already paid to the estate agent. If you cannot afford the full deposit your solicitor may be able to negotiate a lower one with the seller's solicitor.

When you pay the deposit to your solicitor he sends a cheque to the seller's solicitor who holds the money, acting either as a stakeholder or an agent for the seller. If he acts as stakeholder he must hold the money in a separate client account, and he is not allowed to pass the money on to the seller without your permission.

If you are involved in a chain, the seller's solicitor will often ask for permission to hold the deposit as agent for the seller. This means that the solicitor does not have to keep the money until completion but can release it to his client, without your permission, so that the seller can use your money as a deposit on his next purchase. This would mean that there is no guarantee that you will get your money back if the sale falls through for reasons beyond your control. This procedure is more common in the north of the country than the south, although it is becoming more commonplace.

How your solicitor can help

Your solicitor can give you guidance as to how you should finance your deposit and he can also help you to raise the finance. There are several options open to you:

1 You have already saved enough money with a building society or bank. In this case, if your account is on notice of withdrawal, for instance 30 days, don't forget to give due notice so that you won't lose valuable interest, and make sure that you have a cheque for your solicitor by the due date.

2 You are a first time buyer and you haven't saved enough to cover the deposit. You can ask your solicitor to try and negotiate a smaller percentage. The contract will stipulate a 'normal deposit' and although this is normally defined as 10%, the seller may settle for less, though probably with a minimum of 5%.

If the seller insists on the full 10%, your best bet is to arrange a bridging loan. If you have not already done this, or you don't have a bank account, your solicitor may well be able to point you at a friendly bank manager. Before taking on a bridging loan you should be very certain about the prospect of completing as soon as possible after exchange of contracts because the longer it takes, the more expensive your bridging loan becomes at 3 to 4% above base rate.

3 If you are selling and buying your solicitor may be able to arrange a reciprocal deposit with the solicitors of other sellers in the chain. In other words, all deposits, regardless of the cost of each property, will be for the same amount and merely 'passed up the line' so to speak, in each case being held by the receiving solicitor as agent for the seller.

4 The fourth option is the Deposit Guarantee Scheme, which has been running for almost two years (March 1985). Although some solicitors are reluctant to operate this scheme, the majority do. This means that instead of having to raise the money, your solicitor will arrange a guarantee for the amount which is sent to the seller's solicitor at exchange of contract. It is not free, it would cost you £28 per £2000, but it is convenient.

On completion

On completion, usually 28 days after exchange of contracts, your deposit will be released to the seller, if you have not agreed to an earlier release. If you have taken out a bridging loan to cover the deposit until your mortgage is released, your solicitor, to whom the mortgage money will have been sent, will pay off the loan directly to your bank. If you are selling and the completion day is the same, your solicitor will release your seller's deposit, if he has not already passed it on up the chain.

The draft contract

The draft contract is prepared by the seller's solicitor once your offer has been accepted. You will have exchanged names and addresses of your respective solicitors with the seller or his estate agent. The seller's solicitor will send what is called a draft contract to your solicitor. It is only a draft contract because your solicitor will want to check it through and, as a result of his preliminary enquiries, he may wish to amend the contract.

A contract is a legally binding document which, when exchanged with the seller, commits you to the sale. (There are certain exceptions to this for which proviso is made in the contract). Therefore, it's very important that your solicitor satisfies himself completely as to every aspect of the contract and what it entails. He won't personally inspect the property and, as all he will have to go on to begin his enquiries will be the draft contract and the agent's particulars, it will help him if you can tell him about any obvious peculiarities you may have noticed about the property.

Contents of the contract

Most contracts are standard printed forms which, when completed, contain the basic information constituting the terms of the contract:

- The names of the seller and buyer
- A description of the property
- The sale price
- Standard conditions which stipulate the rights and duties of both the seller and buyer
- Any special conditions

The conditions will include details of how much deposit should be paid at the exchange of contracts, and how it is to be paid, eg, bankers draft, cheque; whether you have agreed to buy any fittings in addition to the sale price, etc. The special conditions will include the contract rate.

Contract rate

This is a very important point as it could cost you! If you delay in completing your purchase beyond the agreed date and are to blame for the delay, you will have to pay the seller compensation. The size of this compensation will be fixed by the contract rate, eg, 5% above base rate of the balance of the purchase price for the period of default. Alternatively, the seller can sue for damages. If the seller himself is in default, the buyer is at liberty in appropriate cases to rescind the contract and call for the return of his deposit or sue for damages or for performance – ie calling on the seller to honour his bargain.

Completion date

You and your solicitor will probably not have decided on a completion date at this stage as there may be too many imponderables to enable you to fix it, eg, when the mortgage advance comes through, the sale of your current property (if applicable) etc. So, the contract will normally state that the completion should take place on the 28th working day after exchange of contracts. The draft contract will also state which banks are acceptable for bankers drafts with which to pay the balance of the sale price. All the cleaning banks are acceptable and, if your account is with a foreign bank with a branch in the UK, this will be acceptable as long as the seller agrees.

Withdrawal from the contract

Another special condition which might be included in the draft contract grants you the right to withdraw from the contract after exchange and to recover your deposit if certain adverse matters come to light after exchange. However, there are several provisos as well.

Types of ownership and title

The seller has to say in which capacity he is selling the property; as beneficial owner or trustee. This means identifying the promises he is making to you when he transfers the property. The type of title will be stated as being either registered or unregistered.

Vacant possession

You will want to be assured that the property is being sold to you with vacant possession and that it will be empty when you move in. You won't want any nasty surprises such as previously undisclosed lodgers or sitting tenants appearing out of the woodwork!

When the wording in a contract is agreed by the two sets of solicitors, they each prepare a final copy of it; this copy is called an engrossment. The contracts will then be ready to be exchanged.

Exchange and completion

When your solicitor is completely satisfied with the contents of the contract, he will let you know that he is ready to proceed with the exchange of contracts. What this means is that there are two identical copies of the contract: you sign one copy and the seller the other – the two are then exchanged. The contract is legally binding once exchange has taken place. You are then committed to the purchase and if you withdraw now you stand to lose not only your deposit but you can be sued by the seller as well. If that sounds rather frightening or gloomy, don't worry, your solicitor wouldn't have let you travel this far down the road if there were any problems which would necessitate your withdrawal from the contract.

Before exchange

Before contracts are exchanged, you and your solicitor will have to be completely satisfied on these points:

- The replies to your solicitor's preliminary enquiries have been made and agreed
- The local land charges certificate and local authority search have not brought any problems to light;
- Your surveyor has carried out a structural survey and his report is satisfactory
- If it's a newly-built house, an NHBC agreement has been received
- Your mortgage will be forthcoming and you have confirmation of this in writing
- You have the funding for the 10% deposit ready (or whatever is agreed) to hand over to your solicitor
- You or your lender have arranged to have the property insured
- The date of completion has been fixed
- And finally, but by no means least, you are absolutely sure that you want to go ahead with the purchase. It would be expensive to withdraw now, but it would cost you far, far more if you changed your mind after contracts have been exchanged.

The exchange

Your solicitor will either send the contract to you in the post or, if it's convenient, ask you to call into his office to sign it. You then return the contract with your cheque for the deposit to your solicitor. He will send the contract you signed to the seller's solicitor to keep and the seller's solicitor will send the copy that his client has signed for your solicitor to retain.

After the exchange and before completion

Completion means the transfer of the property to you and the purchase money to the seller has taken place. On the day of completion, the seller has to leave your new home and remove all his property other than what he has agreed to sell you.

However, there are certain matters which must be attended to after you have exchanged contracts and before completion. This means that there's usually a period of about four weeks between the time that contracts are exchanged and the day of completion. While you are busy arranging practical matters, such as organising the furniture removers and packing up, your solicitor will carry out the following services for you:

Proof of ownership

The seller's solicitor will have to prove his client's ownership of the property so that the title can be correctly transferred to you. He does this by supplying your solicitor with copies of the entries on the land register; the filed plan and any documents which have been noted on the register; the authority to inspect the register (your solicitor would not be allowed to make this inspection without the authority); and if he hasn't already supplied them before the exchange of contracts, he'd now have to produce copies of any documents which create or show evidence of rights which affect the property which don't appear on the register.

When your solicitor is satisfied by his examination of the title he will send some further questions about the title to the property to the seller's solicitor. This is called Requisitions on Title. This also includes questions that will finalise details about how and when you will be able to obtain the keys, whether everyone currently living in the property has agreed to leave it on the big day, and so on.

Final searches

Another search has to be made at the Land Registry to make sure that there has been no change made on the register since the office copies were issued by the Registry. If the title is unregistered a search has to be made at the Land Charges Registry to make sure that the seller is not bankrupt. Arrangements will also have to be made for the mortgage lender's solicitor to make searches on his client's behalf.

Exchange and completion (cont)

Lender's enquiries
Your building society or other lender will make some final enquiries to your solicitor which are again called Requisitions on Title. They will want to receive confirmation from him that you will be obtaining vacant possession, making up the balance of the purchase money out of your own funds (unless some form of top-up mortgage has been agreed), that you won't be sub-letting to anyone, who else will be living in the house with you (eg, your spouse), the completion date, and a list of documents that they will require to be handed over by completion.

Discharge of seller's mortgage
If your seller has a mortgage on the property this will have to be paid off on completion. This is to make sure that there is no other financial claim on the property, other than your own mortgage, when the property becomes yours.

Apportionment of rates
The seller will have to give his solicitor receipts for rates, water rates and any other outgoings, for instance ground rent or service charges, which have been paid up to a date beyond completion so that he can apportion some of the cost to you.

Completion statement
The seller's solicitor will draw up a completion statement and send it to your solicitor. This will set out exactly how much money he expects you to pay on the day of completion. This will normally be the purchase price, less deposit(s) you have already paid, plus any proportion of rates, etc. The form will also request the way in which the money is to be paid. This is usually by banker's draft but quite often, when the money is being used to purchase another property, a telegraphic transfer is used so that a chain of completions can take place on the same day.

Completion day
This is the day when you complete your purchase. Your money is paid over to the seller and the keys to your new home are yours!

You will have to be financially prepared before completion so that your solicitor has the money on his account to forward to the seller's solicitor. Your mortgage loan will have been sent direct to your solicitor. If you have a mortgage on the home you are selling, this will be discharged by your solicitor and he will hold any balance to be used towards the purchase of your new property.

You will also have to have made available any other finance such as a top-up loan, bridging loan and personal savings.

Your solicitor will have asked you to send a cheque to him for this balance at least three days before completion so that the cheque can be cleared by the bank. Alternatively, you can arrange with your bank to send him a banker's draft, which is signed by a bank official and is irrevocable.

You don't have to be present at the actual completion transaction. More often than not this will be done by telegraphic transfer or postal transfer between the two solicitors. The title deeds or land certificate will be kept by your mortgage lender as proof of their security.

The seller's solicitor will have agreed with your solicitor by what time the property must be vacated and where you can pick up the keys to your new home. If these have been left with an estate agent, he will not release them until he has had confirmation from the seller's solicitor that the transfer has taken place.

There now only remains the matter of your solicitor's bill, which he will probably present to you within a few days of completion. The two single largest items will be his fee and the stamp duty, but it will also include the costs of the searches, the Land Registry fee and your solicitor's disbursements.

You are, we hope, home and dry.

Stamp duty/solicitor's disbursements

When you come to pay your solicitor's bill just before or just after completion, it will include entries for stamp duty, searches, registry fees and disbursements, as well as his fee. If you have to pay stamp duty, it may be the equivalent or more than the solicitor's fee.

Stamp duty

Stamp duty is a form of words for a property purchase tax. It is not levied on property purchases under £30,000 (at start of 1987), but once you exceed that magic number you have to pay 1% of your purchase price. For example, if you buy a home for £50,000 you will have to pay stamp duty of £500.

The figure is set by the Chancellor of the Exchequer in the Budget. It doesn't, by any means, change with every budget but, as property prices have risen sharply in 1985 and 1986, the threshold may be increased to take this rise into account. There is nothing to stop a government from increasing stamp duty in bands, rather like income tax. For instance, a government could introduce a 2% tax duty on property purchases over £100,000. However, this is not the case at the moment – stamp duty is 1% of the purchase price over £30,000 (at start of 1987), however expensive the property and regardless of which tax band you are in.

Can you avoid paying stamp duty?

The short answer is 'no'. However, if you have put in an offer for a property which is just above the £30,000 limit, you may be able to come to an arrangement with the seller whereby part of the price includes fixtures and fittings, bringing the sale price of the bricks and mortar to below £30,000 and thus not being eligible for stamp duty. This is perfectly legal and your solicitor will be able to advise you on this point.

How stamp duty is paid

When you come to complete and your solicitor presents his bill, it will include an amount itemised as stamp duty. Within 30 days of completion, your solicitor will have to send the deed of transfer of your property to the Inland Revenue with a cheque for the duty payable. They will then make an impress stamp to show how much stamp duty you have paid, and a second impress acknowledging the fact that the Inland Revenue have seen the transfer document. If you didn't pay the duty you would be fined and your ownership of the property wouldn't be registered with the Land Registry.

Following completion, your solicitor will send you a statement of payments and receipts recording all your financial transactions and the balance due. In this example Mr Smith has sold a flat to Miss Brown and bought a property from Mr and Mrs Green.

MR J. SMITH
to
BLOGGS, BLOGGS & BLOGGS
As to your sale of 103a, Park Street,
Parkstown and purchase of
64, Square Avenue, Squarestown

	Payments	Receipts
By *Miss Brown*		
Sale price		29,000.00
Proportion of ground rent paid in advance		4.11
Proportion of insurance premium paid in advance		20.83
To *Parkstown Building Society*		
Amount paid to redeem mortgage	10,759.49	
To *Squarestown Estate Agents*		
Commission and VAT	667.00	
To Cheques sent to you	17,598.45	
By Cheque from you per *Squarestown B. Soc*		3,895.00
By *Squarestown B. Soc,* mortgage advance		35,533.00
To *Mr & Mrs Green*		
Deposit paid	3,895.00	
Balance purchase money	35,055.00	
By *Mr & Mrs Green* allowance for water rates		.60
To *Inland Revenue* stamp duty on transfer	390.00	
To *H M Land Registry* registration fee	60.00	
To *Squarestown Council* search fee	14.40	
To *Land Charges Registry* search fee	.50	
To *Bloggs, Bloggs & Bloggs*		
Law costs, VAT and disbursements	661.25	
By Balance due to Bloggs, Bloggs, & Bloggs		647.55
	69101.09	69101.09

Considering the pitfalls

Needless to say, there are occasions when things don't go as smoothly as you would wish them to. You may have heard stories from friends and acquaintances of gazumping, broken chains, withdrawals of offers and so on and the frayed nerves, heartbreaks and despair which the victims suffer as a consequence. We hope that it won't happen to you but if anything does go wrong with your purchase, your solicitor should be able to steer you through the hard times.

These are some of the pitfalls to watch out for:

Gazumping

This is a very unsociable practice which is born of greed and often condoned by less scrupulous estate agents. It occurs most often during property booms when property prices are rising weekly and there are plenty of buyers in the market chasing too few properties. What happens is this. Mr and Mrs Smith are property hunting and they find just the home they've been looking for. Mr Brown, the seller, is asking £40,000 and so the Smith's put in an offer for the full asking price. Mr Brown accepts their offer and both solicitors are given instructions to proceed.

However, Mr Brown allows his estate agent to continue showing prospective buyers round his home and two weeks later another couple put in a higher offer than the Smiths', for £43,000. Mr Brown tells the Smiths that unless they can match the offer he will accept the second bidder's and they will have to withdraw. The Smith's can only afford £40,000 and have to withdraw, they have been gazumped. They have no protection under the law as no contract has been exchanged.

Withdrawal of offer

If you are selling a property, you'll probably feel enormously relieved when you are offered the full asking price and you accept. Everything is proceeding apace and then you are suddenly faced with the buyer's withdrawal from the sale. This can be very aggravating if you have put in an offer on another property and you've suddenly got to start again. This can happen for a number of reasons: the survey on your property has been far from complimentary (you may be able to negotiate a lower price, if you wish to, under these circumstances): the buyer can't get a mortgage; or he may have gone on viewing other properties and found one which he prefers to yours. Again, if this happens before contracts are exchanged, there is nothing you can do and you'll have to put your property back on the market.

Chains

This can be a nightmare situation where, through no fault of yours, delays along the chain can result in you losing your sale or being unable to buy the property for which you've made an offer. Theoretically, a chain can start with a flat and spiral upwards to a mansion. All it means is that as a person sells a property he also tries to buy another. Seller number two is also trying to buy and so it goes on, with perhaps four or five sales linked together in a chain, each dependent on the success of the other.

This is a situation in which you have to hope that your solicitor is a magician who's good at juggling. Synchronisation of timing is terribly important as far as exchange of contracts and completion is concerned. If you all exchange simultaneously, deposits can be moved up the chain. If you all complete on the same day, seller's capital can be used towards the purchase of the next property and so on. It also means that you can all move on the same day, saving the expense of storing furniture and perhaps having to take out a bridging loan.

If one person breaks the link it can play havoc. This can happen if there's a bad survey on one of the properties, finance isn't available, or one of the people involved in just taking too much time so that the whole process grinds to a halt. You can help yourself to a certain extent if you're in a chain by keeping in regular contact with the seller/buyer on either side of your link in order to anticipate problems.

Contract races

Sometimes a seller who wants a quick sale and who is in a position to receive several offers on his property will instruct his solicitor to send out draft contracts to several people who have put in offers, with the proviso that the first to exchange wins.

This encourages risk taking as, in order to get ahead, you might forego a full structural survey and some of the searches as both these processes take time. Your solicitor will advise you to weigh these risks very carefully before entering a contract race. If you win by cutting corners you could regret it. If you lose you could end up with a large bill and nothing to show for it. Most solicitors will advise against becoming involved in a contract race if at all possible.

DIY conveyancing

The pros and cons of doing your own conveyancing are many, and only you are in the right position to judge whether you can 'go it alone'. The most obvious advantage of not having a solicitor to do your conveyancing is the saving you will make, between about ½ to 1% of your sale price or purchase price. The other side of the coin is that if you do it yourself, you stand to lose a lot of money if anything goes wrong. A solicitor has professional indemnity insurance to fall back on, you don't.

You can always ask for advice from a friend who may have done his or her own conveyancing in the past. They will be able to point out the pitfalls and whether they found it worthwhile. Having said that, it's worth bearing in mind that buying a property can be a fraught business at the best of times and the additional responsibility of taking on the conveyancing could turn out to be the straw that breaks the camel's back. Even solicitors sometimes ask their colleagues to do their own conveyancing on their behalf. It's an old proverb in the legal profession that a lawyer who acts for himself has a fool for a client!

Remember, too, that if you decide to use a solicitor or conveyancer, shop around for a good deal. As solicitors no longer have the monopoly in the conveyancing market, there is far more competition which is reflected in the fees.

The cons

1 If you are about to buy a newly-built house, forget any thoughts of doing your own conveyancing. The contract will prove to be very complicated because it is being issued for the first time so all sorts of issues have to be proved. For instance, that the house is built properly, where the boundaries lie, access, restrictions, etc.

2 If the property is unregistered (not entered on the land register) leave the conveyancing to a professional because you would have to research the deeds and titles back over a period of at least 15 years, and know what defects to look for.

3 Leasehold flats and maisonettes also have complications because of the provisions of the leases which have to deal with the shared facilities and obligations such as maintenance, insurance and repairs. The preliminary enquiries and investigations would have to be exhaustive and are much better left in the experienced hands of a solicitor or conveyancer.

4 You do not have professional indemnity insurance which a solicitor does and a conveyancer should have. This means that if through a conveyancing fault of yours, the sale misfires, you may be liable to pay the seller's and other related costs.

5 Finally, if you are hard-pressed at work or you have several other commitments, it may be worth paying a solicitor to take the strain, as doing your own conveyancing can be both time-consuming and worrying.

The pros

1 It can be a very straightforward exercise to do your own conveyancing. All the necessary law forms can be bought at legal stationers shops and there are plenty of excellent and practical guides available to steer you through the various stages. All you will need is patience and the ability to pay attention to detail.

2 The best position to be in if you are going to perform your own conveyancing is if you are buying a second-hand property situated in England or Wales, which has a registered title whose current owner is the owner-occupier who doesn't intend to do his own conveyancing.

3 As we pointed out earlier, you stand to save yourself at least ½ to 1% of the sale price if you don't have to pay a solicitor or conveyancer. You will still have to pay Land Registry fees, search fees and stamp duty (if applicable) and your own disbursements such as telephone calls, stamps, and so on.

4 If you are in the position of not having to get a mortgage to pay for your purchase, there is a strong case for DIY conveyancing. As a solicitor has to be involved where a mortgage is concerned, you would end up paying for, say, the building society solicitor.

5 If you are doing your own conveyancing, you will always be aware of how far the sale has progressed. You won't have to be in constant touch with the solicitor – often having to chase him – and you may be in a position to improve the timing where searches are concerned and to chase the seller's solicitor.

Buying and selling in Scotland

Scottish law is different from English law which prevails everywhere else in the UK (except for the Channel Islands where Norman Law is used, which is outside the scope of this book). The legal terms have different names and, in some cases meanings – for instance freehold doesn't exist in Scotland, most properties are owned in 'feu' which may lay down certain conditions on the buyer. The process of buying property in Scotland differs somewhat as well.

In Scotland, most property is offered for sale through solicitors' property centres. Estate agents have only recently started to open up shops north of the border, whereas in England and Wales it is quite the reverse.

Finding a solicitor

If you wish to buy property in Scotland you will need to engage the services of a Scottish solicitor, who will be familiar with the whole procedure. If you are living in England, an English solicitor who has previously dealt with Scottish solicitors may be able to provide some useful contacts. Otherwise you should ask friends, colleagues or a Citizens Advice Bureau for their recommendation, or the Law Society of Scotland (see **Useful addresses** [pp. 188–189]).

Although the stages of property purchasing are very similar to those in England, they don't occur in quite the same order.

Prices

Properties are advertised with an 'upset' price, which means that offers above that figure will be accepted. This is, if you like, tendering for the property because you're putting in a blind offer. For instance, the 'upset' price may be £30,000 and you put in an offer for £31,000 but someone else may bid higher. Similarly, all other bids may be £30,000 so you would have paid £1,000 above the odds. With his local knowledge your solicitor may be able to give you guidance, especially if his practice sells property which is very common in Scotland.

Surveys

In England it is common to make an offer for a property, subject to survey. In Scotland the reverse is true: you don't make an offer until you have had a successful survey report. This may mean that you have to pay for surveys on several properties before you are successful, but many surveyors may restrict their fees if you have to use their services on several occasions.

The offer

This is a far more formal affair than in England, usually in writing by your solicitor according to your instruction. Rather like a draft contract, it will be a detailed offer in which you stipulate how much you want to pay, when you want to move in and what, if any, contents you want to buy. If more than one offer has been submitted the seller's estate agent or solicitor will compare the offers, taking not just the price into account but the moving date and contents price as well.

If your offer has been successful, your solicitor will be notified of the fact within the hour and the contract negotiations begin between the seller's and your solicitors. At this stage, you are still not legally bound to pursue the sale. Local authority searches will be carried out by your solicitor – in Scotland these generally only take a few days – and if these are satisfactory, the final letter of contract (known as 'missives' in Scotland) will be sent by your solicitor to the seller's. This is the same as exchanging contracts in England, with the same legally-binding consequences. One substantial difference, however, is that you won't have had to pay a deposit, which makes sorting out your finances less of a headache.

If you are obtaining a mortgage, your solicitor will report to the lender about the title of the property and arrange the mortgage documents which in Scotland go under the name of 'a standard security'.

The settlement

Completion day in Scotland is called 'settlement'. Your solicitor will have arranged for your mortgage funds to be sent direct to him and you will have provided him with a cheque for the balance. He then hands over a cheque for the entire price for the purchase of the property and contents to the seller's solicitor in return for which he will receive the title deeds, conveyance and the keys. He will record this and the mortgage in the 'General Register of Sasines' (Scottish titles register) for which you will have to pay a fee plus, of course, stamp duty as in England.

SECTION SIX

PREPARING TO MOVE

The first priority when you know you will definitely be moving is to set the exact date of the move; then you will be able to plan everything else to fit in with a specific timetable. Your solicitor and the seller's should have arranged a general time for completion; tell them any dates that are particularly suitable or unsuitable, and they should be able to liaise with the seller to fix a date that suits you both. You may find that it's impossible to move out of your present property and into your new one on the same day; if you have to vacate your property first you will need somewhere to stay and somewhere to store your furniture; if you can move into your new property first you will need a bridging loan to cover the extra capital you have tied up for those extra few days. Normally, though, you will be vacating one premises and taking up residence in the new one on the same day.

Once the date has been fixed, the next important item to sort out is the workforce. This is not so much the removal men as the help of a few willing friends. If you are using a removal firm it's ideal to have two people, either members of your household or close friends, at each end on the day of the move. Of course, if you are doing all the removal work yourself you will need a few more friends who are not only willing but strong! If at all possible, make sure that younger children and pets can stay with friends for the day; it will be less traumatic for all concerned this way. Children from about age 15 upwards will be able to provide valuable help during the move without getting too tired.

Service arrangements

Check that you inform gas, electricity and telephone offices of the date of your move, and book anyone that you will need to work on your appliances on the day, for instance to disconnect a gas cooker or an electric wall heater. Confirm the date too with the same organisations at the other end, and make it clear that you will only be responsible for bills up to the moving date at your old address and from the moving date at the new address. Cancel your milk and paper deliveries at your old house, and arrange them to begin at your new one. Fill in a change of address form at the Post Office so that they can forward your mail (there is a charge for this service), and send out change of address cards to your friends, bank, insurance brokers, etc. It's best to send these out in advance, saying that from such-and-such a date your address will be different; you will have plenty to do just after the move without writing to all your correspondents.

Sorting things out

It's never too early to begin sorting out the contents of your property; most of us hoard more than we would believe possible when we actually get it out into the light of day! Especially go through the attic, trunks, under-stair cupboard(s), boxroom(s), shed(s) and garage(s), and decide what you are going to get rid of. There are five main ways of getting rid of unwanted goods: give to friends; sell (either to people you know, to second-hand shops, or through advertisements in your local paper); give to a jumble sale or charity shop; throw out for the dustmen to take; or (with larger items) take to a rubbish tip. Use the list below to write down items as you go through the house room by room, then dispose of all the items in each section at once where possible.

Give to friends:

Sell:

Give to jumble sale or charity shop:

Throw out:

Take to rubbish tip:

Using removal men or DIY?

There are, of course, pros and cons in relation to all types of removal, whether you do everything yourself, hire a van and a little help, or pay a removal firm to do everything for you. The different factors you will need to balance up will be:

- How much you can afford
- How much there is to move
- How many heavy or awkward pieces you have
- How many valuable or fragile objects you have
- How strong you are
- Whether you have easy, cheap access to a van
- How far you are going
- How many helpers you can muster
- Whether you can bear the thought of doing it all yourself
- Whether there will be several small children around
- How much time you have to do packing in advance.

Look at all these points in the light of the suggestions below, and come to the conclusion that will best suit you, your household and your pocket.

Moving yourself
You will need to obtain a van from somewhere, either by borrowing from a friend or by hiring. In both cases you will need to check very carefully the position on insurance for yourself, the van, and its contents. If you are going to do the driving yourself, you can drive a van up to 7.5 tons laden weight on an ordinary licence, but even that can be an enormous amount if you're not used to driving big vehicles, and a van of this size may not be as big as you need. For anything larger you (or a friend) need an HGV licence. Vans are usually available for hire by the day/weekend/week with unlimited mileage, or at a lower rate plus a set amount per mile, so of course you will need to balance up how far you are going with how many trips you will need to make and how long you will need to hire the van for.

One of the main advantages of hiring a van yourself is that you can pack and unpack at your own pace; if you are moving only a short distance you can load the furniture from one or two rooms, drive to the new property, and get those rooms sorted out before you do the rest. This may be particularly helpful if you are in a fortunate position of being able to move over several days, but of course you will need to hire the van for the extra days as well.

A workforce is something that will be vital if you do all the work yourself; how many willing, strong friends can you muster,

and will they all be available on the day? Moving yourself is not particularly advisable if you have several small children who can't be left with anyone else; everyone's tempers will become frayed with the long, tiring work and the different demands for attention. Be prepared for very hard work, and be realistic about the energy and the length of time needed to carry all your furniture and boxes to the van and into your new house; try actually moving a piano or a freezer before you make any rash decisions! Of course, it is silly to arrange to move yourself if you are pregnant, or have a bad back, or are generally in poor health, unless you can find someone to do the bulk of the work for you. The main advantages of moving yourself are that it is (or can be) cheap, and that you can pack your belongings at your own pace.

A man and a van
Local papers often advertise men with their own vans who will help you move. The advantages and disadvantages are similar to those above, with a few extra points. Again you will need to check the insurance position carefully, and you will still be expected to do all the packing (and possibly all the lifting) yourself.

Removal firms
This is the traditional way to move. Removal firms are specialists, of course, and so should be able to avoid pitfalls that you might fall into if you move yourself. They will cost you quite a lot of money, but you will need to offset this against their greater experience and speed, the time and effort they save you, the cost of hiring your own van, and the fact that there should at least be some insurance cover on any goods that are damaged in transit. You may find that it's possible to do a half-and-half deal with a removal firm, for instance with you packing everything and them loading and driving it; they may even supply tea chests and packing materials in advance to enable you to do this. In any case, if you use a reliable removal firm you should be able to feel happy that they have taken a lot of the hard work off your shoulders.

Choosing a removal firm

If you look in your local directories, you will find that removal firms of all sizes abound. How on earth do you go about choosing one? The best way is by personal recommendation; if you know that a friend whose judgement you trust has used a firm that he or she found efficient, quick, clean, cheerful, helpful, uncomplaining and reasonable in price, the chances are that you will be similarly satisfied by the same firm. If you have a large number of delicate or valuable pieces of furniture or other belongings to move, you may be advised to get a recommendation from a local antiques dealer, who should know of reliable firms used to dealing with that kind of load needing extra-careful handling. If all else fails, consult Yellow Pages.

Estimates

It's important to get several estimates so that you can compare prices, but don't get so many that you have to spend all your preparatory time showing foremen around your house: 3 or 4 is probably ideal. Try and make sure that all the firms you consult are members of the British Association of Removers, as this organisation insists that its members use well-maintained vans and good crews, and also will deal with any problems if they arise (see **Useful addresses** [pp. 188–189]). They also have reliable insurance schemes (see pp. 144–145).

Estimates will depend on how much stuff you have to move, and how far you are going; they may also vary, in some firms, according to your exact moving date, with Fridays, Saturdays and school holidays being more expensive. Some firms may be able to fit you in as a part-load if you don't have much to move, which will be considerably cheaper than having to pay the full amount for hire of a van.

It's important that you show the estimator from each firm *exactly* what needs to be moved – including items from the attic, shed, garden, outhouse(s), garage, etc. It's also important that they have reliable details of your new house.

Factors that might alter their quotation include:

- How many floors there are in your new house
- How many rooms there are
- Whether there are any extra-low or extra-narrow doorways
- Which floor in a block a flat is situated
- Whether there is a lift in a block of flats
- Whether there is parking nearby
- Whether there are any traffic restrictions on the road (eg, no heavy lorries)

- Whether there is a long front path
- Whether there is easy access to the back door and garden
- Whether the internal stairways are narrow or steep
- Whether there is a spiral staircase
- How near the van can get to unload.

The more of this information you are able to provide, the more accurate the estimate will be. You will also need to negotiate, and possibly ask for a separate estimate, if you want to pack all the items yourself, or a considerable proportion of them. Remember though that an estimate is just that – a rough idea of how much the move will cost. Once you have chosen your firm, ask for a fixed quotation; this then cannot be altered except in writing.

Choosing

You won't necessarily want to choose the cheapest quotation; if one firm will make you carry all the goods yourself, or you didn't like the general appearance of their men or van, you may well be better off choosing the next most favourable quotation. If you are moving from a large town to a small one you may well find that you will get a considerably better quotation from a firm in the smaller town; plenty of firms will need to move a load from Smalltown to London, so you will only have to pay for the return journey, but not many firms will find a load that needs to go from London to Smalltown.

Confirmation

Once you have made your choice, confirm the order by telephone and then in writing, setting out clearly the relevant dates, venues and times; ask the removal firm to confirm in writing in turn. Check also that you are both agreed on exactly what is being moved; if there are any major alterations (for instance you decide to sell the cooker instead of taking it, or vice versa), ask for an amended quotation. Read the small print carefully too, to check that the price quoted included suitable insurance and VAT. Most removal firms ask for payment in advance, but this is undesirable; it's sensible not to pay until the move has been completed to your satisfaction. Ring the removal firm a day or two before the moving date, just to check that everything is booked as planned.

Travel insurance

Insuring the goods you own during the move is vital, but is easily overlooked in all the other preparations made during the process of buying and moving house. Many people assume that a removal firm will automatically provide cover for anything damaged during the move, but this is not necessarily the case.

Insurance through the removal firm

Always choose a firm that is a member of the British Association of Removers (see **Useful addresses** [pp. 188–189]), as their members should provide adequate compensation for items damaged during the move. An added bonus is that if your removal firm goes bust while your goods were in transit, but was a member of the BAR, the Association will arrange for another member firm to complete the move at no extra cost.

Check your particular firm's insurance arrangements carefully. Although many provide insurance, if you read the small print you may discover that they pay out not on the value of the goods damaged but on the amount of space taken up by them in the van, and the sum paid out may be as little as £5 per cubic foot! Generally, good removal firms will undertake to replace any items they damage, or to provide compensation if replacement is impractical. You may, of course, find yourself arguing about the value of objects damaged; sentimental value is difficult to put into terms that are recognised in the commercial market-place.

It's also important to check the firm's policy on insuring goods that you have packed yourself. Some firms will include this in their own cover; others will specifically exclude it, and others will pay if it can be shown that the firm's employees subjected the boxes or cases to extraordinary damage, such as dropping them downstairs or allowing them to fall off an improperly-loaded lorry. Valuable items are a bit or a problem, especially if they are irreplaceable. Do you want to take the risk of the removal men packing them, with their greater expertise, even though their insurance wouldn't cover their full responsibility for their packaging and transport? This is an equation that you will need to work out for yourself.

Taking out your own policy

The best way to make absolutely sure that your belongings are covered by insurance during the move is to take out an extra policy to cover the transition. You will almost certainly find that the firm that arranges your normal property contents insurance will be prepared to extend this cover to insure the goods while they are being moved. The advantage of this scheme is that your property contents will probably already be well-documented by your insurance firm, so you should be able to obtain a reliable quotation very easily; you may find, however, that this payment may then load your premium payments in the future. Another method is to ask the removal firm to arrange a policy for you, which they will probably be able to do; they are likely, however, to build their own cut into the premium quoted. Alternatively, you can ask an insurance broker to give you a quotation for a temporary policy to cover the move. Whatever policy you finally settle on, check the small print. You may be happy with a general cover of £10,000 to cover all the contents, but the details may specify that there is a ceiling of, say, £500 on any one item. That's not much use if it's your £800 stereo or £1200 fur coat that's been damaged.

Checking for damage
Before the day of the move itself, take a long hard look at your furniture and make a mental note of any noticeable damage such as scuffs, scrapes, tears, stains, chips and so on; it's most unfair to blame removal men for marks you just haven't noticed before! As the furniture is unpacked at the far end, make a surreptitious inspection of its condition – it's a little tactless to inspect the goods openly in front of the men as they carry them in. If you do notice any damage which obviously wasn't there before, such as a cracked mirror or a crushed corner on a bookcase, point it out politely to the foreman of the team. If possible, unpack fragile items before the workmen have finished so that if any glasses or china are broken you can also bring them to the foreman's attention. Send a letter immediately to the removal firm, detailing the damage, and requesting suitable compensation to be deducted from your total bill; this is why it's important not to pay out in advance! If you have had to pay in advance you may find that the firm is extremely reluctant to refund the money you're owed, so make sure as far as possible that your case is well-documented, for instance that other members of your household can confirm that the damage was done during the move. If you do have any problems claiming from a member firm, write to the British Association of Removers giving as many details as possible (see **Useful addresses** [pp. 188–189]).

Notifying everybody

Of course many of your friends and relations will know that you are moving, but it saves a great deal of trouble if you send out change-of-address cards – otherwise people tend to write the details down on scraps of paper and then lose them! You can have

Friends	Relations

cards specially printed fairly cheaply, or you can buy 'blanks' at a stationers' and simply fill in your new name and address. Use the lists below to jot down names of people you must notify (you may need to photostat them if you have a large family or lots of friends.

People at work

....

....

....

....

....

....

Bank(s)

....

....

....

....

Insurance company(ies)

....

....

Building Society(ies)

....

....

Premium bonds

....

Car insurance company

....

DHSS

....

Employer(s)

....

....

Book club(s)

....

....

Mail order catalogue(s)

....

....

Clubs and associations

....

....

....

Other firms or organisations

....

....

....

....

....

....

Packing when using removers

Even if you have hired a removal firm to do most of the work for you, there may well be some items still that you would prefer to pack yourself. Of course, it's also possible to arrange with the firm that you do part of the packing, for instance of specially valuable or precious items, and that they do the rest; they should be able to provide an amended quotation if you want to do this, and may even lend you tea-chests and packing materials in advance.

Jewellery is one of the items that most removal firms insist you pack yourself; this makes sense when you think that jewellery is likely to be among your household's most valuable possessions, and also is the kind of item most likely to be tempting to weak-willed removal men! If you have a great deal of jewellery, buy some special dark baize from a jeweller's and pad it with that; generally your ordinary jewel case will be sufficient outer protection, and can be slipped into a box with other things that you are taking to the new property in your own car. You may also prefer to pack other valuable items yourself, such as pictures, priceless glasses or ornaments, special collections, silverware, wines and spirits, or special light fittings.

It will help the removal men enormously and save time if you pack small items into cardboard boxes so that when they arrive they don't have to wrap every item individually. This kind of item includes things such as make-up, cleaning things, etc, from the bathroom and kitchen, herbs and spices, stationery, sports equipment, tools, gardening items such as seeds and plant-pots, and items such as kitchen tools.

Before you move you will need to make various other preparations that will make the removal firm's task easier. Empty out messy things such as chip pans, petrol from motor mowers, earth from garden tubs or window boxes. If you have a freezer remember that it may need to stand at your new house without being switched on; also, on long journeys, the food in it may defrost. Therefore it's better to run down its contents in the preceding weeks, preferably to nil. If you're taking items such as a gas or electric cooker, an electric wall fire, or kitchen units attached to the walls, it will make moving day an awful lot easier if you have the preliminary work done one or more days beforehand. You may also want to pack your clothes yourself, although some removal firms have special wardrobe bags and will pack and unpack your clothes as part of the service. The checklist on the opposite page will help you to plan in advance the items you will have to pack yourself, even when using a professional removal firm.

What to pack in advance	5 days before	4 days before	3 days before	2 days before	1 day before
Jewellery 1					
2					
Other valuable items 1					
2					
3					
4					
Wines and spirits 1					
2					
Pictures 1					
2					
Small items 1					
2					
3					
4					
Things that need emptying or cleaning before the move 1					
2					
3					
4					
Work that needs doing before the move 1					
2					
3					
4					

Moving yourself: choosing the van

So – you've decided to be brave and move yourself! You'll need to do a bit of forward planning to check that everything is going to run smoothly on the day. The first item you'll need to sort out is the van that you'll use for the move.

Vans from hire firms

As with removal firms, there are numerous firms that are only too keen to hire you vans of different sizes and capacities. A browse through your local papers or telephone directory will provide probably dozens of suitable firms. You'll probably find it best to choose medium-to-large firms; they have the advantages that they should have a range of vehicles to choose from, should be well-covered by reliable insurance policies, and should have plenty of vans in good working order so that there are back-ups if anything goes wrong with the van you have booked. You may wish to avoid the very large national firms; if the people manning the desk don't have a personal interest in you as a customer, you may find that queries and complaints can only be dealt with by head office. On the other hand, very small firms may be unrealistically expensive, or may lack the back-up facilities of larger ones.

Once again it's often best to go by personal recommendation if at all possible; if you know someone who has been satisfied with the service provided by a particular firm, then it's likely that you will be satisfied too. If you don't know anyone who can give you a personal recommendation, approach three or four companies and ask them for quotations to cover your needs.

If you've never moved yourself before, you may find it hard to estimate the size of the van you need, or that you will feel comfortable driving. Decide whether you would prefer a large van for only one load, or a smaller one for two or three trips. You may find that the firm will be willing to let you test-drive two or three different vans to see how easy you find them to handle. Remember that you will need an HGV licence to drive any very large vans; even for a small van you will need a clean driving licence.

Ask to have a look at examples of the vans hired out, and see whether they look as though they are clean, well-maintained, reasonably modern, and generally in good condition. Check the exact terms of the contract, the insurance cover, what time you can pick the van up and when it has to be back, and the size of the deposit you will need to leave; some firms will insist on the deposit being in cash.

Vans hired from individuals
If you are hiring a van and a driver, ask if you can go round and talk to him and take a look at the van. Once again, check that it looks reliable and well-maintained. If you are using this scheme you will be particularly open to problems if anything goes wrong on the day, for instance if the driver is ill or the van breaks down; check whether there is any back-up service in these cases, and if so, ask for the details in writing. Check too the exact charges, and whether these are inclusive of insurance and VAT. Ensure that both of you are agreed on when and where you are meeting, where you are driving to, and how long you think the job will take.

Finance
Although hiring your own van, either from a firm or an individual, should be cheaper, it's worth itemising the expenses that will be incurred just to check that this is in fact the case – and so that you won't be faced with any nasty surprises on the day. Use the list below to help your budget.

Charges for hiring van, or van and driver	
Insurance, if extra	
Extra rate for mileage (multiply by two for the round trip, then multiply this sum by the number of trips you will have to make)	
Petrol	
Total transport costs	
Deposit: how much is it, and does it have to be in cash?	
What time can I pick the van up, and from where? time: .... where:	
What time do I need to return the van, and to where? time: .... where:	

Moving yourself: packing

If you're moving everything yourself, you have a unique opportunity to spread your packing over days, weeks, even months before the moving day itself. Make the most of it! As soon as you know that you are going to be moving, stock up on dustbin liners and other large, strong plastic bags; cardboard boxes (raid your local supermarkets); tea chests, if you have a local source; and old newspapers.

Order of packing

1 First of all, pack non-essentials; but make sure that they actually *are* non-essential. For instance, it's no use packing your sports kit if you remember that you're playing in a badminton tournament the week before the move. Generally, though, you can begin packing weeks before the move as long as you choose carefully. First things to pack might be books, records, tapes, items related to hobbies or collection, pictures, ornaments, some garden tools, sewing machine, winter clothes if it is summer (or vice versa).

↓

2 Then, as the move approaches, move on to more important things; just leave enough for the final few days. Pack most of your clothes and shoes, most plates, cutlery, non-perishable foods and kitchen utensils, hi-fi, spare bedding, other tools. Disassemble any fold-down furniture, beds, etc; you can always sleep on mattresses on the floor for a few nights!

↓

3 Finally, on the day itself or the previous day, pack everything that's left; of course, large items such as chairs and table won't actually be packed in anything, they'll simply be loaded into the van.

Method of packing

Remember that items such as books, crockery, casseroles and bottles are very heavy; be realistic about the number that can be packed into a cardboard box, which might have been manufactured only to carry even smaller lightweight boxes of cereal. It's much better to pack lots of small boxes than to over-fill a large or medium-sized one and have the bottom fall out.

Clothes can be loosely folded and packed down into large plastic bags; the same applies to spare bedding, pillows, sleeping bags and other soft furnishings such as curtains and rugs. Seal the neck of each bag with masking tape so that the contents don't spill out when you're carrying them. These large soft bags can be used to pad larger pieces of furniture when you're packing the van, and are also very useful for filling up spaces such as in between the legs of tables and chairs.

Fragile items should be wrapped individually in newspaper; this takes a long time, but is well worth it in the long run as the risk of breakages is much less. Hollow items such as glasses should also have a ball of newspaper or tissue paper placed inside them so that they are less likely to break. Mark boxes 'Fragile' and 'This way up' so that the friends helping you will know which boxes to take extra care of.

Be very careful of items that are irregularly shaped or which have protrusions, for instance the knobs on stereos, or delicate lights or lampshades. Where possible, pack the spaces around these items with soft things such as rags or, failing that, newspaper.

Large items such as garden tubs, window-boxes, shelves, garden chairs, etc, are probably best left unpacked, and just stowed in the van on the day; trying to find boxes large enough to take them will be difficult, and would be very unwieldy anyway. Use the tables below to draw up your own order of packing

First stage (during the weeks before the move)

....	....
....	....
....	....
....	....

Second stage (7–2 days before the move)

....	....
....	....
....	....
....	....

Final stage (the day before the move, and the day itself)

....	....
....	....
....	....
....	....

Plans for your new home

It's sensible to make a simple plan of your new home well before moving day. This will not only be invaluable on the day, but will help you to sort out beforehand just what will go in each room, and even what order you need to do your packing and unpacking in. Number the rooms on all floors, and any other major sites, such as a garage, greenhouse, shed or lean-to, which will need objects moved into them. Once you have done this, make a set of large cardboard numbers to be fixed on the door of each room in the new house on moving day, corresponding to the numbers on the plan. Then there should be no confusion! Buy several large sticks of chalk, and as you or the removers pack each box, draw the appropriate number on the box or tea-chest of the room that it will go to; chalk can also be used safely on most furniture and other large objects, such as plant tubs and waste bins, and will rub off later.

Well before you move, make plans for priority jobs to be done in your new home. Then whoever is at the other end can be getting on with them while they wait for the removal van to bring the furniture. This scheme also applies if you are moving over several days; you will then have that much more time to get each room sorted out before you need to fill it with furniture. Use the table below to work out your own list of priority jobs for your new house.

Priority jobs

....	....
....	....
....	....
....	....
....	....
....	....
....	....
....	....
....	....

Plans of your new property

Use this page to draw simple plans of each floor of your house, and any outbuildings you will need to move things into. The drawings don't need to be large, or even to scale; just show where each room is and the position of its door. Give each room a number, and allocate a number too to any other spaces such as hallways, landings, under-stair areas, back patios, etc; these will then correspond to numbers on your packing cases when you move. Make several photocopies of this list.

The night before the move

Inevitably there will be numerous last-minute arrangements to see to, even though you will at this stage feel as though you have been working up to the move for months! If you can get lots of these arrangements done on the day before, though, you'll find that you'll leave yourself as free as possible on the day itself.

This may be the day that you've set aside for disassembling furniture such as bookshelves, beds, self-assembly wardrobes, greenhouses, garden furniture, etc. Check that you have several copies of your property plan ready to give to appropriate people as you begin the move, and make your cardboard numbers for the doors of the new rooms if you haven't already done so. Make sure too that your chalk is handy for marking packing-cases.

Take a look around all the rooms and ensure that everything that should have been sold, given away or thrown out has been; if not, make some emergency arrangements! Make sure that you have handy some money, your cheque book and other important documents relating to the move, the phone numbers of your removal firm, solicitor, new property, and seller's solicitor, and also some coins for phone boxes; things have a habit of going wrong when you're nowhere near your own phone! Also double-check any letters giving details of times (for picking up the van, removal men arriving, picking up the key to the new property, etc) and costs (for van hire, van deposit, removal firm, petrol). If you will need to leave a cash deposit for a van in the morning, check that you have the necessary money. Pack up and check your box of essentials (see pp. 172–173).

Food

This will be a priority during the moving day! The previous evening is an ideal time to make an enormous batch of sandwiches; don't underestimate the appetites of all of you, householders and removal men alike, when you're involved in so much hard work. Also keep to hand items such as fruit, cake, biscuits and chocolate bars that can be used to boost the morale and the blood sugar level at regular intervals. You'll also need, of course, supplies for the inevitable steady stream of cups of tea and coffee. Cold drinks will be welcome too, so lay in some cans or mix up a batch of squash and buy some plastic or paper cups so that you don't have to keep on washing up.

Cleaning

Although it seems like something you could do without, in the middle of all the other arrangements for moving, a thorough clean of the property you're leaving is essential. Of course, some touches will have to be left until the last minute, such as vacuuming the carpets (there's no point in doing this until all the furniture has been moved), but most of the heavy cleaning can be done in previous days and checked through the night before.

Areas to be cleaned

Use the list below to check that all areas have been covered; tick them when they're done.

- [ ] Kitchen
- [ ] Utility room
- [ ] Hallway
- [ ] Living room
- [ ] Dining room
- [ ] Other reception rooms
- [ ] Study
- [ ] Cellar
- [ ] Downstairs cloakroom
- [ ] Main bedroom
- [ ] Bedroom 2
- [ ] Bedroom 3
- [ ] Bedroom 4
- [ ] Bedroom 5
- [ ] Playroom
- [ ] Bathroom
- [ ] Toilet
- [ ] Landing
- [ ] Other bathrooms
- [ ] Loft
- [ ] Shed
- [ ] Other outside buildings

Any other areas

- [ ] ....
- [ ] ....
- [ ] ....
- [ ] ....
- [ ] ....

Moving abroad

One move that you can't do yourself is when you are required to transport your belongings abroad; there are so many documents and special arrangements needed that only an experienced firm can ensure a smooth transition. Choose a removal firm that specialises in moving abroad, and check that they are members of the BAR Overseas Group (see **Useful addresses** [pp. 188–189]). They will then be well-qualified to advise you on what to take, how to go about it, etc. They should also guarantee you a quotation for door-to-door transportation; door-to-port will be cheaper initially, but will involve you in possibly ruinous arrangements for storage and transportation when you get to the other end. Firms moving goods abroad require payment in advance, as they will often have to pay out themselves for shipping and handling. This can be worrisome when your personal effects are disappearing into the blue, but if you ensure that your removal firm is a member of the BAR-IMMI scheme, the BAR will guarantee to have your removal completed satisfactorily or refund your payment, even if the original firm you booked goes bust while your goods are in transit.

Specialist firms will be able to advise you on what to take abroad with you and what to leave behind. To some extent this advice will depend on the particular country you are moving to; for instance, it's unlikely that you would be able to take your current car to America because of their exhaust regulations. Certain countries will forbid you to take in books and magazines which you may consider harmless, but which might transgress their laws on decency. Some countries will forbid you taking in house plants because of the risk of disease; others are very suspicious of cane furniture for the same reason.

Other advice applies to most countries abroad. First of all it's important to check the availability and prices of general items such as furniture, electrical appliances, beds, carpets and so on. If the prices are very low then it's not worth the expense of shipping your own goods over. Do most of the houses where you will be living have gardens? If not, it's not worth taking all your garden tools, garden furniture, mower, etc? Do most of them have built-in cupboards? Again, if so, you should leave behind wardrobes and most other storage units. If you are moving to a hotter country you will almost certainly require a much larger fridge and freezer than you currently have, so the expense of shipping your own over will be prohibitive. If you are moving into a well-established network of British expatriates, for instance the Forces, NATO, the British Council, large firms, etc, you may well find that it's customary to save the expense of removals by buying household effects and furniture from the people whose jobs you will be taking over.

There are a few things, however, that it might be prudent to buy before you go. If you are considering making a major expenditure, for instance a car, a washing machine, a hi-fi system, a computer, etc, you may well find that you will be able to purchase the goods free of VAT if you are staying abroad for a year or more. Once again your remover, of the BAR, may be able to advise you.

Once you have decided exactly what you are taking with you, make a very detailed inventory. It's important that there are no discrepancies between this and the goods that are going through customs, otherwise you will incur delays at least, and possibly heavy fines into the bargain. Your remover will liaise with a remover abroad and arrange all the documentation you will need to transport and ship your goods. They will be sealed into a container, in their packing cases, and opened officially by the customs officers at the destination country. The fee you pay your removers will not include any customs duty incurred, or storage costs if there is any delay. It's very important to make sure that your insurance covers your goods for the whole journey – while they are in transit, in storage, and in the hands of customs.

Customs clearance generally takes 10–14 days if all goes smoothly, although, of course, numerous factors can cause delay – strikes, overwork, discrepancies in the documentation, etc. Customs policies vary enormously from country to country; again, a specialist firm should be aware of the general routine in your destination country. There may be particular regulations relating to specific goods; for instance in Australia any television sets will be taken away and tested to make sure that they are compatible with regulations. In Canada the owner of the goods is expected to be present during the procedure of customs clearance. Make sure that you know in advance just what will be expected of you, and when, and where – will you need to report to a dock, to a customs warehouse, or to be at a particular office on a particular day?

One final word – before your goods are shipped, which will often be a number of weeks before you travel yourself, make sure that you have kept with you all the documentation you will need; it's easy for some of it to be packed along with less important papers. You will want to keep passports, insurance certificates, visas, inoculation and vaccination details, any documentation relating to your present and future accommodation, and of course to the move itself.

Putting belongings into store

You may find, for one reason or another, that it's necessary to put your belongings into store. This quite often happens if it's been impossible to synchronise exactly the dates of moving out of one property and moving into your new one; you may find that you are committed to sell your own property before you have finalised details of the new one, or that you have to move down and begin a job by a particular date and you don't want to have to return to the other end of the country in a few weeks' time to oversee a move. You may know exactly how long your goods will need to be in store, or it may be an indefinite period dependent on how long it takes you to find a property, or when a brand-new property is ready for occupation.

Most of the guidelines are the same whether your goods are to be in store for a week or so or for a matter of months. First of all, choose a reliable company for storage, preferably going on personal recommendation if possible. Most removal companies have, or can liaise with, storage facilities themselves. Ask to look round the depository so that you can assess for yourself whether it looks suitable or whether it is simply an empty warehouse, etc, that has been temporarily commandeered. See whether the place looks, feels or smells damp, whether it is musty, draughty, etc, and whether it seems weather-proof.

It's always sensible to wrap any valuable items that might deteriorate left exposed to the air – fur coats, valuable carpets and rugs, paintings, etc. Check exactly what the insurance position is: is there any limit to the claims that could be made in the event of any damage? Would the claims be limited to a particular ceiling per item, for instance £500? Or would you simply have to make a general claim? Make absolutely sure that your insurance covers any reasonable eventuality, such as fire, flood, theft, etc. Moths can be a problem even in the best depositories, so use anti-moth sprays and mothballs liberally among clothes, curtains, carpets, etc.

If you have a fridge or a freezer, you must of course empty it completely while your goods are in store. It's also important to wedge the doors open if you possibly can; the seals on fridges and freezers are so good that if they are left closed, detached from a power source, mould will grow in a matter of days. No perishable items of any sort should be left within your goods, for instance foods such as rice, cereals, sugar, etc; quite apart from the risk of attracting vermin or mould, the goods will almost certainly be unappetising if not downright inedible when you collect them from the store.

You should also make sure that there is nothing easily flammable among your possessions, and nothing potentially explosive (this will probably be one of the conditions on your storage agreement, in any case). Goods of this sort include firelighters, oils (eg, car oil), mowers containing petrol, gas cylinders (for instance for camping stoves), table cigarette lighters, firelighting briquettes, etc. It's also advisable, because of the potential fire risk, not to leave any aerosols or perfumes in store. No firearms or ammunition should be put in store – these present a security risk as well as a fire risk. If you have any houseplants, it's much better not to put them in store – even if they are the kind that generally thrive on neglect? It's much kinder to them to ask a friend or relative to look after them; then even if your goods have to be in store for longer than you originally thought, you'll know that your plants will be in good condition.

You may know when you make the storage arrangements exactly what day you will want the goods to be released, or you may know the week; check exactly what charges will be incurred, and what the arrangements will be if, for some unforeseen reasons, there is a delay and the goods have to stay longer. On the other hand you might be storing the goods indefinitely, for instance until you find a suitable house; in this case make sure that you know what the charges will be per week so that you're not faced with an unexpectedly large bill at the end of the storage period.

If there are any other goods that you know, or suspect, you will want ahead of the others, ask the storage firm for some 'Keep forward' labels so that you can attach them to the items or boxes concerned. Then, when the firm is arranging your goods in the depository, they will place these so that they have fairly ready access to them. Getting particular goods out from among all your household effects, if you suddenly remember that you need something specific, can be costly otherwise.

Once you know when you will need your goods out of store, give the firm several days' notice. Remember that they will need to provide a van, a driver, and the men to shift the furniture out of the store into the van, and these won't necessarily be available at last-minute notice. Check everything as it is unloaded at its new destination, and follow the guidelines for general removals; if anything is damaged, point the fact out to the foreman, and inform the firm in writing as soon as possible.

SECTION SEVEN

THE DAY OF THE MOVE

The two most important things to remember to make the day of your move easier are: to have all the people where they are meant to be, and to have all the things where they are meant to be! It sounds so easy, but will of course be the culmination of months of planning. If you are moving out of one property and into another on the same day, which is the most common state of affairs, you will want to finish up at the end of the day with you, your household (children, pets, etc) and all your belongings safely ensconced behind your own – new – front door, with nothing left at the old property and nothing and no-one lost or damaged on the way. You may feel that you've done enough planning, list-making and thinking ahead by this stage, but just a little bit more will help to turn the day of the move from a potential nightmare into, ideally, a smooth transition. Of course no-one can guarantee fully against such things as cars breaking down, appalling weather conditions, or sudden hold-ups in the legal completion of the sale, but certainly you can take steps to make the day as trauma-free as possible.

People

You should have decided well in advance who will be where on the moving date, and how they're going to get there. Don't forget to make arrangements for the transport of whoever stays in the previous property overseeing the move; the removal men aren't going to want to make room for 'one more inside' in their van! The person who is going to be at the new property should set off in good time, armed with the box of essentials (see pp. 172–173), the cardboard letters or numbers for the rooms of the new house (see pp. 154–155), a plan of the property, a tool box, and any items that you may have decided you would like to move yourself. He or she should be well armed with sandwiches and drinks, information such as addresses of solicitors, where the keys can be collected, etc, and money and cheque book if necessary. Make sure, though, that the first person to leave doesn't take everything; you've still got a long day ahead of you in the old house, and you too will need a kettle, cups, food, and possibly money to cover any unforeseen expenses which might arise.

If you are farming out children and pets, arrange for them to be collected as early as possible (or ideally the night before) so that they are not too upset by the inevitable air of change and disruption. Check with the removal men the time that they think they will be finished, and arrange to pick up the children and pets (or have them delivered) at a suitable time.

Packing
Despite all your sorting in the previous days, whether you are packing up your own things or not there are things which you can only do on the last day. These are also usually things that you will be needing very quickly once you get to your new house, so make sure that they are clearly identifiable and are packed somewhere obvious in the van so that you can get at them when you need them. Keep aside one, or several, large plastic bags, ideally transparent so that you can identify them at a glance, in which to pack the bedding you have used the night before; one of the first tasks you'll want to do in the new home is to make the beds up. If you can't find transparent bags, make a large distinctive label and tie it firmly onto the bag.

Use another bag, also well-identified, for your nighties or pyjamas, washing items, towels, hairbrushes, basic make-up, and so on that you will need for the first night and morning in your new location. You won't want to be searching around among all the boxes and bags for these items. Also try and make sure that a complete change of comfortable, crease-free clothing is ready to hand; moving is a very grubby business. Choose casual, loose-fitting, hard-wearing clothing for the day of the move; jeans or tracksuits, or something similar, are ideal. Food will be another important consideration for the first few days after the move. On the morning of the move pack all the breakfast things, such as cereals, toaster, marmalade, etc, into one box so that they're ready for use on your first morning the other end. Think through what you're going to do about an evening meal at the end of the moving day; if there is a take-away restaurant near you then this is probably the ideal solution, but check that it will be open on the day you move, and that you have crockery and cutlery for eating the food. Even if your cooker is going to be connected the day you move in, you still won't want to be bothered with cooking a complicated meal, so plan something simple and straightforward. The main concern is to have lots of food; moving is hungry work.

Finally, make sure that you keep by you in the old house anything that you will need to clear up after all the packing is done; brushes, cleaning fluids, cloths, sponges, washing-up liquid and, of course, a vacuum cleaner. Once you've got all these items sorted out, you should be ready for the move itself!

The legal side

Despite all the forms you've worked your way through, interviews you've had with building societies and solicitors, phone calls you've had with estate agents, vendors, removal firms, etc, there are still legal considerations that are of vital importance on the day of the move itself. It is most common for completion – as its name implies, the final part of the property sale and purchase – to take place on the day of the move. You are not legally allowed in before completion has taken place, so it's important to check shortly before the day of the move first of all whether there are any potential hold-ups, and secondly exactly what time completion will take place as, strictly speaking, you will not have access before that time to your new property and you will want to avoid the possibility of removal men, etc, turning up early.

You may find that the present owner of your new property will let you in a day or two before the sale, for instance to have a carpet fitted, or to paint some of the rooms. This is more likely to happen if the property is currently standing empty; the seller is not likely to want to be interrupted in his or her own removal plans by you arriving to put up some curtains! However, it is entirely up to the seller whether you do have any access, and his or her solicitor will often advise against it, as there may be legal complications, so don't count on having this kind of access.

It's important too to check completion time, and to tie it in with when you or your representative will be in the house, so that you can inform any people that are coming to do work in the house on moving day. For instance, if you are having new lino laid in the kitchen you want it done before the removal men arrive with the cooker, fridge, washing machine, etc; on the other hand, you don't want to keep them hanging around outside the house for several hours if there is a hold-up on completion. Keep handy the phone numbers of any firms that are involved in this way on the day of the move; early on moving day ring your solicitor (if he or she hasn't already rung you) and confirm that completion is going ahead as planned. If there are any delays, you can then make alternative suitable arrangements with the workmen involved. Your solicitor should have confirmed before the day of the move exactly when the keys to the new property will be available, and where they can be picked up from. Decide who is going to pick them up and at what time; the person concerned should then immediately check that he or she has all the relevant keys, for instance front and back door, garage, shed, side gate, summerhouse, any internal doors.

Organising the timing

Use the spaces below to fill in information that should help to make the day of the move as uncomplicated as possible.

Property

....

Date of move ....

	Time schedule
Estimated time of completion	
Time keys will be available and place keys can be picked up from?	
Who will pick up keys and at what time?	
What time will the removers arrive at the old property?	
What time will the removers arrive at the new property?	
What time do we have to be out of the old property?	
Will anyone be arriving at the new property during the day to work on it? If so, who, and at what time? .... Phone numbers	
What time will children, pets, etc, be delivered?	

Last-minute things to do

Inevitably there are some things that just have to be done on the day of the move itself. You want to make sure, obviously, that you take everything with you that is yours, but it's just as important to make sure that you leave in your old property everything that you said you would, and that you leave it safely – even if the property is only going to be empty for a matter of hours.

Once you've packed all your obvious last-minute things, such as washing items, nightclothes, make-up, bedding and breakfast things, you can begin checking the house for other things that need doing before the removal men arrive or before the new owners move in. You may need to dismantle things such as self-assembly wardrobes or shelves, or this may need to be done as the removers pack away the contents. Some furniture has to be partially dismantled to make sure that it can go in through a narrow doorway or up a steep staircase; you may also find that it takes up less room in the van if this is done before you arrive at the new property.

It will save the removal men time, and probably make unpacking easier at the far end, if you pile together things such as cushions from armchairs, loose seats from kitchen chairs, shelves from bookcases, canisters from the bathroom and kitchen, etc. If you haven't said that you will be leaving them, you can busy yourself removing lightshades and bulbs, and any light-fittings that you are taking with you, and curtains and curtain-rails. You may even be taking your carpets, but taking up carpets is heavy work so leave it to the removal men if you prefer.

Safety is important; as the property empties, check the different parts to see that all the appliances are in a safe condition. Of course you don't want to turn off the heating or the hot water until the last minute if possible, but check that all unused powerpoints are switched off, that the immersion heater isn't on, and that there are no appliances such as fires left plugged in or switched on. You will probably have arranged by this stage to have your gas or electric cooker disconnected; if it isn't being done until the moving day itself, check that there are no wires left exposed and so on. If the property is to be empty even for a day or so during the winter it is often a good idea to turn the water off at the mains – but do leave an obvious note for the new owners telling them where the stopcock is!

Things to do on the last day:

- [ ] Strip beds
- [ ] Pack bedding
- [ ] Pack nightclothes
- [ ] Pack washing items
- [ ] Anything to dismantle?
- [ ] Light-fittings
- [ ] Curtains
- [ ] Curtain rails
- [ ] Carpets or floor coverings
- [ ] Cooker disconnected?
- [ ] Gas appliances turned off?
- [ ] Electric appliances turned off?
- [ ] Boiler turned off?
- [ ] Water turned off?

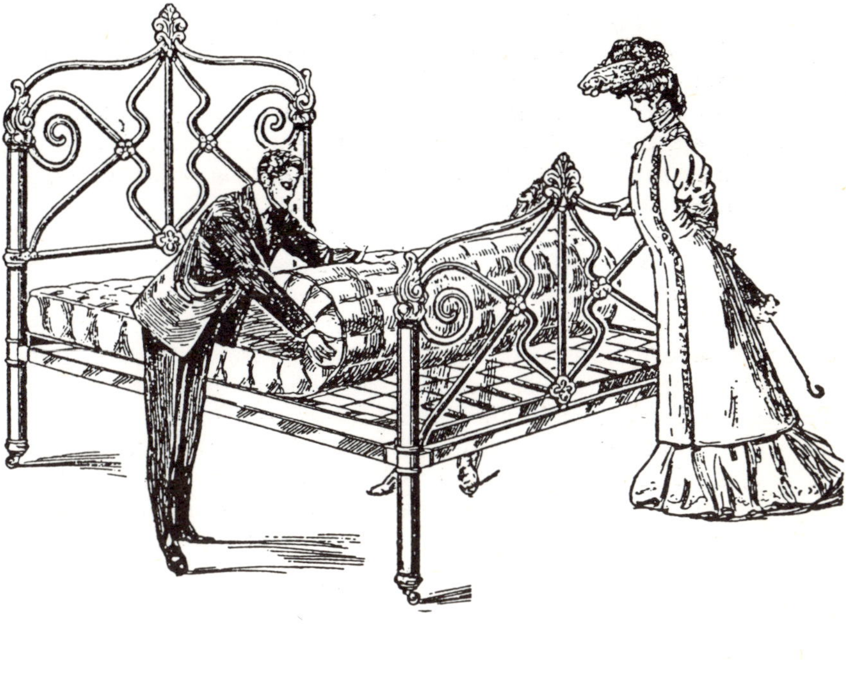

Packing your own van

If you have decided to move yourself, you may well have done all your packing bar some last-minute items in the preceding days and weeks; this will only leave you with the task of actually installing all the goods in the van in a sensible fashion. On the other hand you might have left yourself with quite a bit of work still to do; if this is the case try and enlist an army of willing helpers, because it's astonishing just how long it takes to pack the contents of drawers, cupboards, shelves, sideboards and wardrobes into the relevant plastic bags and boxes.

If possible, arrange to pick up the van well before you want to start loading it so that you can give it a good look over before the move and, if necessary, change it for a more satisfactory one. Check that the brakes, tyres, oil and water levels, etc, are OK; even if it is morning when you pick it up you may well be driving it later in the evening, so check at this stage that all the lights (headlights, sidelights, indicators, reversing light and hazard lights) are working well. It's advisable to walk round the van with a representative of the hire firm before you drive it away, just so that you are both agreed on what marks, dents, etc, are present already when you begin to drive it. If you are hiring a large van it should come with a sturdy ramp to help you get the furniture onto the back; take the ramp out and check its condition, and ask for a demonstration of exactly how it fits onto the back of the van. See how much petrol there is in the van, and top it up to the level you are likely to need for the journey or journeys ahead of you.

As well as the van, you will need some other basic equipment to help you load. If you can borrow a porter-type wheeled trolley you will find it invaluable for helping to transport large, heavy items such as fridges and settees, as well as for boxes of books and other goods that may strain your back. You will also need plenty of rope, and ideally straps and stretch fittings, for making sure that your load is really secure. If you are hiring a large van that will mainly be used for removals, you may find that it comes with these, but having some more at hand won't go amiss. Rope in particular will always be handy; the more secure your load is, the easier the van will be to drive – and the safer your goods will be too, of course.

Order of packing

If you are packing the van yourself, the order is very important; don't just put things in at random. You may also feel that it's logical to start with the larger items and then fit the smaller ones around them, but in fact this is just the wrong way to go about it.

You need to pack the van in the reverse order of the order in which you will require the items at the other end. So, for instance, in the new property you will want the living room carpet before you will want the three-piece suite. Use this flowchart as a rough guide, adapting it to suit the contents of your own property.

1 Small and light articles, such as the contents of the kitchen cupboards, ornaments, toys, clothes, cutlery, china, light-fittings, curtains, pictures

2 Somewhat heavier things such as books, records, shelves, garden tools, electrical appliances, mower, children's bicycles, sewing machine, paints and other DIY stuff, plant tubs, hi-fi

3 Small items of furniture such as bedside cabinets, coffee tables, dining chairs, cupboards, telephone tables, children's bookcases, garden furniture, dismantled self-assembly furniture

4 Heavy furniture such as tables, armchairs, settees, beds, bookshelves, wardrobes, desks, piano, cot, chests of drawers

5 Any floor coverings you are taking with you

6 Last minute things that you might want quick access to at the other end, for instance your bedding, things for an evening meal, and box of essentials if it hasn't already gone on ahead.

The pitfalls of DIY packing

The most important thing to remember when you are packing your own van is to be sensible. It's remarkably easy to damage your back severely, or to crush a finger or a foot badly, if you are amateurs moving lots of heavy items, especially when you are negotiating tricky areas such as steps, stairs, narrow doorways, slippery garden paths, etc. Always take everything slowly and carefully, stop frequently for rests, and make sure that you lift articles properly so that you aren't straining the wrong muscles. *Don't* lift anything at all heavy if you are pregnant, have a bad or weak back, suffer from high blood pressure or any heart complaint, are elderly, or are in poor health. Make sure too that the helpers giving you a hand don't strain themselves – you'd never forgive yourself if one of your friends damaged himself or herself through overzealousness on your behalf.

1 When carrying a heavy object in one hand, hold the other out to the side to balance the weight.
2 Never pick things up in this way, by bending over at the hips and lifting; this puts great strain on the back and can damage it permanently.
3 Instead, when lifting heavy objects bend the knees, grasp the box or item firmly, then (with your back straight) straighten your knees slowly.
4 Take care when you are pushing heavy items; use your back arms or shoulders against the object then straighten your legs to exert pressure. This way your stronger leg muscles take the strain rather than your back or shoulders.

As well as packing in the rough order listed on the previous pages, you will need to check that any very heavy items, such as a heavy bed-frame or a piano, are over the axles as much as possible – either the front axle or the rear one. Pianos are expensive items and often cause great trepidation in the owner's heart. If you prefer, you could probably pay a special piano removal firm to deal with yours; if it is a very good one it may be worth doing this, unless you have sufficient insurance to pay for a complete replacement if it is irreparably damaged. If yours is just a fairly ordinary piano, though, you should be able to move it without too much trouble. If you treat it with respect, keep it upright all the time and handle it gently, you may well find that it doesn't even need retuning. Never lay a piano on its side, back or edge.

Freezers too are a little temperamental; just as with a piano, a freezer should always be kept upright. You may even find that any insurance or maintenance agreement it is under will be invalidated if the freezer has been laid on its back or side. If it's absolutely unavoidable that you have to lay it on its back, for instance if the size of the van simply won't allow for it to be upright, then stand it upright for a minimum of 24 hours, disconnected, to allow the oils to settle to their proper level, before connecting it to the electricity supply at the far end.

Make sure as you pack that you don't put fragile boxes at the bottom; it's easy to miss the chalked notices on the boxes if you are looking for one of a particular size or shape to fill an empty space. Don't balance things precariously either; you could have a scene of chaos when you open the back of the van at the other end if you've piled things haphazardly on top of one another. Use soft items such as sheets, pillows, cushions, sleeping bags, curtains, duvets (all of them ideally in plastic bags) to pad the spaces between furniture and more fragile objects, and tie everything securely in place with ropes, straps and stretchy loops so that the load is as stable as possible. When you're driving, take things slowly, even if you've practised driving with the large van, it will handle very differently once it is full, and you may find it swaying quite a lot until you get the hang of keeping full control. Just be sensible, and don't take risks – with the van, your belongings, or yourself – and you should find that things work fine.

A box of essentials

You can't count on having anything available in your new home; even if there are good shops nearby, you're not going to want to waste time stocking up there straight away – and then maybe having to do several trips because there are things that you've forgotten. It's much better for the person who goes ahead to the new property to take a box of essential (or very useful!) items, so that you've got everything on hand for making tea and coffee, maybe having a simple meal, doing any simple repairs that need urgent attention, cleaning items such as the sink and toilet, and so on. If you have a camping stove, this will ensure that you have the means to boil a kettle, even if the electricity is off. Other items that are worth taking are coins for pay telephones, matches (in case automatic pilot lights aren't working on boilers, cookers, gas fires, etc), towels and soap (you're all going to get very grubby), lightbulbs (in case the previous owners have left you in the dark), things such as a craft knife, string, scissors, sellotape, glue, and a toilet roll.

If you're going to be doing any major work on the house when you arrive, then of course you will need appropriate tools, equipment and raw materials. This work could be as diverse as wallpapering, painting, cleaning out the kitchen cupboards, knocking down built-in cupboards, taking up carpets or lino, building a work surface in the kitchen, or putting up shelf units or curtain rails. Try to keep this work on the first day to absolute essentials, unless the person concerned is going to find that time hangs heavy on his or her hands – which may well be the case if you are moving a long way away, and have to wait a long time for the van to arrive. Maintenance work of this kind is very tiring, and there will be plenty of other work to tire you too when the van arrives! On the other hand, if a room is decorated in unspeakable taste, a coat of paint and a new floor covering will really make you feel straight away that it is yours.

Make sure that the person in charge of affairs at the far end of the move knows exactly when people will be due to arrive to do things such as fit carpets, connect the cooker, deliver a new fridge, etc; this means that he or she can then choose a time carefully if a quick dash to the shops becomes essential.

Finally, if the budget runs to it, pack in a bottle of wine or champagne, so that when you've finally shut the door on the removal men you can celebrate being in your new home!

Remembering what you need

Use this list as you pack your own box of essentials, to ensure that nothing important is left out.

- [ ] Food
- [ ] Cold drinks
- [ ] Teabags/coffee
- [ ] Powdered or UHT milk
- [ ] Sugar
- [ ] Disposable cups, spoons, plates
- [ ] Washing up liquid
- [ ] Soap
- [ ] Towel
- [ ] Cleaning powders and liquids
- [ ] Cloths, rags and dusters
- [ ] Dustpan and brush
- [ ] Mop
- [ ] Broom
- [ ] Bucket
- [ ] Sponges
- [ ] Craft knife
- [ ] Scissors
- [ ] String
- [ ] Sellotape
- [ ] Matches
- [ ] Lightbulbs
- [ ] Coins for the telephone
- [ ] Tool box
- [ ] Camping stove
- [ ] Toilet roll

Any items needed for essential repairs/decoration on the day

....

....

....

Instructing the removal men

Removal men are very experienced, and as far as the packing and actual transportation of the goods goes they should be able to get on with the job very well by themselves. However, every household is different, and you will have certain requirements that are unique to you; the removers will expect you to be concerned about your belongings and have particular ideas about how you want them treated, etc, so don't be embarrassed about giving them a few polite instructions. After all, you are the one who is employing them.

Before the removers arrive, make sure that any boxes you have already packed are marked in chalk with the number or letter of the room to which they are going in the new property; you can also do this with large items of furniture. Then, as they pack boxes, you can mark those boxes too. Also in advance you can make out large 'Do not remove' notices for anything that is staying in the property. Mark with 'Fragile' notices anything that needs special care taken of it, especially if it is something that might not be immediately obvious to the removers – for instance you might have a very valuable candlestick that looks ordinary, a clock that has a very delicate mechanism, or a piece of furniture which has sentimental value.

Agreeing on the task

When the removal men arrive, find out who their foreman is and make sure that the two of you agree on everything that is to be done. Walk round the property and, if necessary, the garden, shed, garage, outbuildings, etc, with him and point out everything that is to be moved and everything that is to stay. Also draw his attention to anything that needs special care. Give him a duplicate list of the items agreed with his firm when they gave you the original quotation, just so that there is no misunderstanding. Make it clear whether articles such as garden furniture, sheds, greenhouses, etc, are to be moved. Point out any dismantling work that will need to be done (remember that this should have been agreed with the firm beforehand), such as self-assembly shelving units, beds, cots, kitchen units, dining tables, cupboards, etc. Show the foreman anything in the loft, under-stairs cupboard or other out-of-the-way place that will need to be moved. If you have any questions yourself, the foreman is the one to ask; he will be more aware of how his company operates, and also more experienced, than the rest of the team.

Helping them out
If the weather is really terrible, for the sake of the people taking on your property next you may want to put down old rugs, dustsheets, etc, over the parts of the floor that the removal men will be constantly walking on – especially the hallway. Remember, though, that there mustn't be any loose edges or wrinkles that they could trip over. Very few removal men will want you to help them pack and carry, unless this has been specifically agreed in the contract (for instance that you will pack fragile or valuable objects while they do the rest). You will usually find plenty of small items to keep you busy, such as emptying kitchen cupboards so that they can pack the contents, cleaning different parts of the house as the removers finish in there, and so on. It will almost certainly be true, however, that the men will welcome the occasional cup of tea or coffee; if this is accompanied by a slice of cake or a biscuit, they may work even harder afterwards!

The far end
Before the removal van leaves, give them a duplicate plan of your new property with all its rooms marked, and check that they understand that the boxes and furniture will go in the rooms corresponding to the numbers or letters they bear. Double-check that they have the correct address of the property they are going to, and also that they have your phone number at your old property, and an official contact number (perhaps the seller's solicitor) at the far end in case there are any problems. When the foreman tells you that they are ready to go, ask him to wait while you go quickly round the property checking that everything that should be staying is still in position, and everything that should have been packed in the van has been. Check how long they think it will take them to drive to the new location, remembering that they may well need to stop for coffee, lunch, to fill up with petrol, go to the toilet, etc, en route. This should then give you their estimated time of arrival at the other end. Once they have set off you can (if the phone has been connected) telephone your partner at the far end, and let him or her know that the removers are on their way and what time they can be expected.

Moving pets and plants

Pets and plants present their own problems during moving. Both require special handling, if they are to survive the experience without lasting trauma!

Pets

The exact method you use to transport your pet will, of course, depend very much on the type of animal, or animals, you have. A stick insect requires very different treatment from a spaniel. Of course, if you have very large or very specialised pets, such as horses, snakes, goats, tarantulas, etc, it's best to get specialist advice from a vet or pet shop on the best methods and conditions of transportation. Most people have more usual domestic animals such as cats, dogs, rabbits, guinea pigs, gerbils, hamsters, mice, etc.

Cats and dogs will vary with their temperament on how well they will take to the move. Most dogs, and some cats, are used to travelling in cars, so it might not be terribly difficult to transport them once you are ready to leave. Even placid dogs and cats, however, will tend to get nervous when they know that a major change is afoot; all the unaccustomed bustle of packing, and all the strange people in the property, will alert them that something is going on.

Some vets will arrange for dogs and cats to be mildly tranquillised during a move; this can save a lot of anguish on the part of both pet and owner. Cats tend to be more difficult to control than dogs when the time comes to get in the car and make the journey, and so a basket may make all of you feel more secure. If you don't own a pet basket, and can't easily borrow one, most pet shops sell very reasonably-priced fold-down cardboard pet boxes that are very sturdy and have their own built-in carrying handles. If the journey is at all long, make sure that your dog or cat has its own blanket, and a small dish of its favourite dry food. Of course if the journey is very long, you'll also need to make careful arrangements for food and toilet requirements. Incidentally, if your cat or dog becomes worked up it may wet the basket, so it's worth lining it well with several thicknesses of newspaper.

Small pets can often be moved in the cages or hutches they generally live in, if they are carefully positioned in a gently-driven car. Large rabbits can also be put into the kind of cardboard carrying box mentioned above. Gerbils, lemmings, hamsters, mice, rats, chinchillas, etc, should all be fairly happy in their own cages; give them plenty of food and liquid to keep them happy.

Don't be tempted to put your pet's cage in the removal van; it will become very lonely and frightened (wouldn't you?), and if there are any delays in the van's arrival you will be worried about its welfare. Also, don't be tempted to pack the cage in the boot; fumes from the car's engine or exhaust might overwhelm or even kill your pet.

Plants

Pot plants can be rather tricky to move, not because of their constitution particularly (they survive all sorts of other neglectful treatment!) but because of their unwieldy shapes (and sometimes sizes). If you have a very large, sturdy plant such as a monstera or rubber plant, you will probably find that the removers can find a corner for it in the van; alternatively you may prefer to take it to its new destination in your own car. Smaller pot plants can easily be crushed, so its best to pack them in groups in shallow boxes; that way they will help to keep each other upright. The removers may have a protected place in the van where they can put your plants; if not, it will be safer to transport them yourself.

If you are taking plants from your garden, remember that you should only take ones that you have specifically said you will to the people who are moving into your property. It's very unfair to them if they think they are moving to a well-established garden, only to find that all the choice plants have gone with you! If you are digging any plants up, lift them the day before if they are reasonably hardy and keep some of the soil around the roots. Moisten the roots well then wrap in black plastic bags to keep the moisture in and the light out. Have a spray bottle handy so that you can refresh the leaves and stems at regular intervals through the next day. If the plants are sizeable, for instance small apple trees, the removers can probably fit them in among the other goods in the van as they are. If they are a bit smaller, pack them in groups in shallow trays or troughs (plant troughs are ideal) so that they give each other a bit of protection, and also help to keep each other moist. Remember, too, that you will need to replant them as soon as possible in the new property, so be quite sure that you can do this practically before you decide to take plants with you. If you want to move herbs, you will probably find that you can transplant them to pots in the days or weeks before your move; then when you get to your new property you can either keep them in the pots or put them out in the garden.

The final check

Once the removal men have driven away, your old home will seem very strange and empty. It will even sound different, with no furniture to cushion the sound and possibly no carpets or curtains either. After all the excitement of packing up, planning your new home and at last feeling that you are now the proud owner of a home elsewhere, you will probably want to get away as soon as possible. Only a final check of your old property is necessary before you can bid it a final goodbye.

It's astonishing just how many things can be overlooked when you're packing, simply because they have been there so long that you scarcely think of them as moveable objects. This is particularly true of pictures, lampshades, clocks, ornaments, even pot plants! Fixtures and fittings can easily be overlooked too; have you taken down and packed things like spice racks, knife racks, tea-towel holders, towel rails, bath racks, soap holders, hanging baskets, wall fires, small shelf units, bathroom cabinets, tool racks, etc? Look carefully too behind any fixtures you are leaving, such as boilers and large cupboards and shelves; all kinds of things may have slipped behind or underneath them, either while you were packing up or before. Look in the bottoms and corners of cupboards, built-in wardrobes and shelves, and on the tops of tall cupboards.

It's only pleasant to leave your property in as clean a condition as possible for the next people to occupy it, so make sure that you have kept a few cleaning materials behind with you – including, ideally, a vacuum cleaner. No matter how house-proud you are, you are bound to find plenty of dust and cobwebs once large pieces of furniture such as wardrobes and bedsteads are completely removed. Have a good sweep through, make sure all shelves and cupboards (especially in the kitchen) are really clean, and vacuum all the carpets.

The final thing to do is to make sure that any relevant information is left in a prominent place for the next owners. It's nice to leave them a note welcoming them to the property, and it's sensible to leave a note of your next address and phone number; they are bound to get a certain amount of mail and phone calls, despite sending out change-of-address cards and having your mail redirected. Ensure that you have left instruction booklets for appliances such as boilers, water heaters, central heating, gas fires, etc, and also let the new owners know if you have turned off the water or electricity. Then you should be all set to make the journey to your new property, knowing that you've left everything in good condition behind you.

Last tasks

Use this list to check that you've cleared everything you should have done and that you've left the property in good condition.

Cleared:

- [ ] Pictures
- [ ] Ornaments
- [ ] Clocks
- [ ] Fixture and fittings
- [ ] Plants
- [ ] Attic
- [ ] Under-stairs cupboard
- [ ] Sheds, greenhouses, garage, outbuildings
- [ ] Cupboards in kitchen
- [ ] Cupboards in bedrooms
- [ ] Airing cupboard
- [ ] Bathroom cabinet

Cleaned:

- [ ] Carpets
- [ ] Lino, etc
- [ ] Toilet
- [ ] Bath, sink, washbasin
- [ ] Cupboards (especially in the kitchen)

First tasks in your new home

When your household is fully assembled at the other end, it would be nice to feel that your work was over – but of course a new task is only just beginning! It's easy to feel a bit depressed, at the end of a day that has been physically and mentally draining, when you arrive at the home of your dreams only to find that it is stacked with partly-unpacked boxes, is full of equally tired people, and that you can't find almost anything you happen to need. Don't let it all get you down though; remember that you don't have to unpack everything and get it in order on the first day – you will have many weeks ahead to sort out the details.

First of all, as you close the door on the removal men, celebrate finally being in your new property with a cup of tea or, if you can afford it, a bottle of wine. This will make you feel a whole lot more positive about the situation! Then, if it's getting near the end of the day, decide what you are going to do about a meal and get this organised; eating something hot and nutritious will also raise everyone's morale. Your first priority as far as furniture goes is to get the beds up and made; you're all going to sleep very soundly after such a long day, and you don't want to have to make your bed at the last minute before you can go to sleep in it. Then your priorities will vary according to your own household and priorities; you may want to get a living room sorted out, so that you have one clear room to use as a haven from the chaos around, or you may feel it's important to get the kitchen clear. If the previous owners haven't left curtains, you will probably need to fix some up fairly urgently (and possibly curtain rails as well). Once you've done the minimum to make the property habitable, don't feel obliged to do everything else as well – there will be many more days to come in which to unpack, sort and fix.

It is important on the first day to go around the property and check, first of all that nothing has been damaged in the move, then that everything the previous owners should have left has been left. If there is anything major missing, for instance if they said that they would leave a cooker or a set of shelves and they haven't, telephone your solicitor the next morning and give him or her details; it is your solicitor's job to chase this kind of complaint for you, even if you know your seller's new address. Make sure also that nothing has been left that shouldn't have been; for instance if the garden is full of rubbish, or the attic is full of broken furniture or old boxes, you will have to pay to have them cleared. Once again, get on to your solicitor if you find anything of this kind amiss.

Finally, once you feel that you're settled in the property and once you have unpacked enough of your belongings to see what's what, go round the property and see what things need doing to it. These might be jobs which are fairly urgent, for instance, if you need to have a window repaired or a banister mended, or they might be long-term, such as painting a room or digging a new flowerbed. They may be small tasks, such as screwing on a new cupboard door-handle, or they may be major such as replacing the guttering or even the roof. Check also whether there are any small things you need to buy for the house within the next few weeks – a toilet roll holder, a towel rail, new batteries for the doorbell, a lampshade, some nails for pictures, etc. Jot down all your findings and thoughts on this page, and you'll have a reminder of what needs doing when.

Jobs to be done

Fairly urgent:

major	minor
....	....
....	....
....	....
....	....
....	....

Long term:

major	minor
....	....
....	....
....	....
....	....
....	....

Items to buy

....	....
....	....
....	....
....	....
....	....
....	....

Glossary of terms

absolute title: absolute ownership of land.

abstract of title: extracts from the deeds of property with unregistered title needed by the intending buyer. It contains proof of the seller's ownership of the property.

advance: the total amount of money provided by a lender.

annual percentage rate: the true interest that you pay on your loan, which takes into account the lender's way of calculating interest.

annuity mortgage: repayment mortgage paying back regularly capital and interest.

assignment: transfer of ownership of leasehold property.

authority to inspect the register: the document by which the registered proprietor allows someone else to be given information about the register of a property, usually to enable him to make an official search.

balance outstanding: the amount left of your mortgage which you owe to the lender.

bank draft: a cheque issued by a bank, which cannot be stopped, and is accepted instead of cash on completion of sale.

bridging loan: a loan, usually from a bank, whereby you can buy one property before selling another.

building regulations: local authority regulations governing the construction of property, such as ventilation, air space, damp-proofing, insulation, etc, aimed at maintaining good habitation standards.

capital: mortgage sum or principal sum outstanding.

capital gains tax: if selling a second home you could be charged this tax on the net profit you make.

charge: a legal term used to describe a mortgage but which, technically speaking, means a liability against the land.

charges register: one of the three parts comprising the register at the Land Registry of a property with a registered title.

completion date: the last stage in selling and buying a property when the balance of the purchase price is paid and documents and keys are handed over.

completion statement: the account of the amount, due to the seller from the buyer, on completion.

collateral: property pledged as a guarantee for the repayment money.

compulsory purchase: effectively compulsory sale. This means that an official body, eg the local council, can force an owner to sell their property under an act of parliament.

compulsory registration of title: the statutory requirement in certain parts of England and Wales that any property, when next bought, should be registered at the Land Registry.

conditions of sale: the detailed standard terms which govern the rights and duties of the buyer and seller of a property, as laid down in the contract which they sign.

contract: an agreement which the law upholds. A property contract details the terms of the sale.

conveyance: the document which transfers the ownership of a property from seller to buyer.

conveyancing: the legal term for transferring ownership of a property or land.

covenant: a promise given in the deed to undertake or to abstain from doing specified things.

deed: the document by which legal title to freehold and leasehold property is transferred.

deed of conveyance: the legal document which transfers the ownership of a property or land from seller to buyer.

delivery: the handing over of a deed with the intention that it should now be operative.

deposit: usually 10% of the purchase price which is handed over when contracts are exchanged. It can be forfeited to the seller if the buyer withdraws after signing a binding contract without good legal cause.

development plan: comprehensive proposals by a local authority for the planning future of areas under its control.

discharge of registered charge: a document by which the mortgagee acknowledges that all the money secured by a mortgage on a registered property has been paid.

draft contract: the document which the seller or his solicitor sends to the buyer's solicitor setting out the conditions of sale.

early redemption: paying off a loan before the end of the mortgage term.

easement: a right over another property (ie right of way, light or drainage).

endowment mortgage: a loan on which only the interest is paid throughout the term and which is eventually paid off with the proceeds of an endowment insurance policy.

engrossment: after a draft document is agreed, the final document is prepared or 'engrossed' for signature.

enquiries before contract: a set of detailed questions about many aspects of a property which the seller, or his solicitor, is generally asked to answer before the buyer is prepared to sign a contract.

enquiries of local authority: a number of questions asked of a local authority on a printed form about a particular property within their area.

equity: the value of a property after all charges against it, eg the mortgage, have been deducted.

exchange of contracts: the point at which the purchase becomes binding in law.

execute: to sign and seal a document.

fee simple: freehold.

filed plan: means by which a registered property can be identified at the Land Registry.

fixtures: articles which, because they are attached to the house itself, as opposed to standing supported by their own weight, are presumed to have become legally part of the house itself.

freehold: the property (mostly houses) is owned absolutely.

good leasehold title: a term used by the Land Registry to describe the possession of title or ownership of a leasehold property which has a registered title, irrespective of the ownership of the freehold or any other superior title.

ground rent: rent paid to the freeholder by the lessee.

interest rate: money charged by the bank or building society for lending money.

Land Charges Registry: a government department where rights over, and interests in, unregistered land are recorded.

Land Registry: government department responsible for registering the ownership of properties.

Law Society: the solicitors' professional body.

law society's conditions of sale: one of the available sets of standard terms incorporated into a contract for the sale of a property which governs the rights of the buyer and the seller.

leasehold: a property is owned for a fixed number of years only.

lessee: the person to whom a lease was originally granted, usually the present leaseholder.

lessor: the original grantor of a lease, usually the present landlord.

letter of acceptance: the document sent in reply to the offer of advance provided by the bank or building society.

local authority: either a district, county or borough council which is responsible for roads, planning, social services and other local matters.

local land charges register: a register kept by the local authority which is consulted at the time of the local search.

mortgage: loan (usually for property purchase) for which the property is the security. It gives to the lender certain rights in the property, including the power to sell if the mortgage payments are not made. These rights are cancelled when the money advanced is repaid with interest, in accordance with the agreed terms.

mortgage deed: the document containing the mortgage conditions.

mortgage term: the number of years over which the loan is to be repaid.

mortgagee: the finance lender, eg, bank or building society.

mortgagor: the person who takes out a mortgage.

offer: the buyer makes an offer to the seller, subject to contract.

office copy: an authenticated copy of an official document issued by the owner of the original. In conveyancing, this usually refers to a copy of the entries in the register of a property with registered title, which is issued by the Land Registry.

overriding interests: rights which are enforceable against a property, even though they are not referred to in the register of the property at the Land Registry.

planning permission: permission from a local authority allowing development. This can cover the addition of extensions, garages, drives, dividing the property, fencing, and so on.

preliminary enquiries: enquiries before the contract is signed.

principal: the amount of the loan on which the interest is calculated.

property register: one of the three parts comprising the register at the Land Registry of a property with a registered title.

proprietorship register: one of the three parts comprising the register at the Land Registry of a property with a registered title.

protection policy: an insurance policy which pays off the principal sum of your mortgage if you die during the term of the mortgage.

real property: freehold land, and any buildings on it.

redemption: the final payment on a mortgage.

register: the record kept at the Land Registry of a property with a registered title.

registered land: land whose title is registered at H.M. Land Registry and guaranteed by it.

registered title: title or ownership of freehold or leasehold property which has been registered at the Land Registry.

repayment mortgage: loan on which part of the capital as well as interest is paid back on a regular basis (usually monthly) throughout the term of the loan.

requisitions on title: questions asked in writing by or on behalf of a buyer about matters concerning the seller's ownership of the property.

restrictive covenants: restrictions applying to the use of the land.

road charges: the charges imposed by the local authority on the owners of properties along a road for the cost of making up or repairing the road, usually calculated according to the frontage of each property. These are only applicable when the road is not a public highway maintainable by the local authority.

scale fee: a fee calculated by reference to the price being paid, rather than to the amount of work involved in a transaction.

seal: a red disc accompanying the signature on a deed.

search: local authority and government department enquiries to find out relevant information about the property.

search certificate: the certificate which states the result of a search.

solicitor's undertaking: a letter signed by a solicitor in which he gives a personal guarantee.

stakeholder: one who holds a deposit as an intermediary between buyer and seller, so that money paid as a deposit may only be passed on to the seller, or returned to the buyer if certain conditions are fulfilled.

stamp duty: tax paid to the Inland Revenue of 1% of the purchase price of a property if it exceeds £30,000 (as at start of January, 1987).

subject to contract: agreed provisionally, but not a binding legal contract: either the buyer or the seller may still back out of negotiations without giving any reason.

survey: can be basic or a full structural survey which is an inspection of a property by an independent surveyor.

tenant: someone who is in occupation of a property on payment of a rent.

tenant for life: a beneficiary who is entitled to receive the rent or other income from, and/or live in, property while he is alive, after which it will pass to others.

tenants-in-common: two (or more) people who together hold property in such a way that, when one dies, his share does not pass automatically to the survivor but forms part of his own estate.

tenure: literally meaning holding, its a term used to describe ownership, eg freehold or leasehold.

title or title deed: evidence of ownership of a property.

top-up loan: a second mortgage taken out when the first mortgage doesn't meet the borrowing requirements.

transfer: the document which transfers ownership of a property with a registered title.

valuation: an assessment made by a lender's representative, eg a local surveyor, to ensure that the value of the property is worth more than the loan applied for.

vendor: the seller of the property.

Useful addresses

Architectural Association
34/36 Bedford Square,
London WC1B 3ES Tel: 01-636-0974

Association of British Insurers
Aldermary House, 10–15 Queen Street,
London EC4N 1TT Tel: 01-248-4477

British Association of Removers
277 Grays Inn Road,
London WC1X 8SY Tel: 01-837-3088

British Insurance Brokers Association (BIBA)
BIBA House, 14 Bevis Marks,
London EC3A 7NT Tel: 01-623-9043

Building Societies Association (BSA)
3 Savile Row,
London W1X 1AF Tel: 01-437-0655

Consumers Association
14 Buckingham Street,
London WC2N 6DS Tel: 01-839-1222

Corporation of Insurance and Financial Advisors (CIFA)
6–7 Leapale Road,
Guildford, Surrey GU1 4JX Tel: 0483-39121

House Builders Federation
82 New Cavendish Street,
London W1M 8AD Tel: 01-580-5588

House Building Advisory Bureau,
12 Crane Court, Fleet Street,
London EC4A 3DB Tel: 01-583-0518

Housing Corporation
149 Tottenham Court Road,
London W1P 0BN Tel: 01-387-9466

Incorporated Society of Valuers and Auctioneers (ISVA)
3 Cadogan Gate,
London SW1X 0AS Tel: 01-235-2282

Institute of Insurance Consultants (IIC)
PO Box 381, 121A Queensway, Bletchley,
Milton Keynes, MK1 1XZ Tel: 0908-643364

Insurance Ombudsman Bureau (IOB)
31 Southampton Row,
London WC1B 5HJ Tel: 01-242-8613

Law Society
113 Chancery Lane,
London WC2A 1PL Tel: 01-242-1222

Law Society of Scotland
PO Box 75, 26 Drumsheugh Gardens,
Edinburgh EH3 7YR Tel: 031-226-7411

London Building Centre
26 Store Street,
London WC1E 7BT Tel: 01-637-1022

National Association of Conveyancers
2/4 Chichester Rents, Chancery Lane,
London WC2A 1EG Tel: 01-405-8582

National Association of Estate Agents
Arbon House, 21 Jury Street,
Warwick CV34 4EH Tel: 0926-496800

National Consumer Council
20 Grosvenor Gardens,
London SW1W 0DH Tel: 01-730-3469

National Federation of Housing Associations
175 Grays Inn Road,
London WC1X 8UP Tel: 01-278-6571

National House Building Council
58 Portland Place,
London W1N 4BU Tel: 01-637-1248

New Homes Marketing Board
82 New Cavendish Street,
London W1M 8AD Tel: 01-580-5588

Road Haulage Association
104 New Kings Road,
London SW6 4LN Tel: 01-736-1183

Royal Incorporation of Architects of Scotland
15 Rutland Square,
Edinburgh EH1 2BE Tel: 031-2297205

Royal Institution of British Architects (RIBA)
66 Portland Place,
London W1N 4AD Tel: 01-580-5533

Royal Institution of Chartered Surveyors (RICS)
12 Great George Street, Parliament Square,
London SW1P 3AD Tel: 01-222-7000

Index